A Poverty of Reason
*Sustainable Development
and Economic Growth*

A Poverty
of Reason

*Sustainable Development
and Economic Growth*

Wilfred Beckerman

The INDEPENDENT
INSTITUTE

Oakland, California

The Independent Institute
100 Swan Way, Oakland, CA 94621-1428
Telephone: 510-632-1366 • Fax 510-568-6040
E-mail: info@independent.org
Website: www.independent.org

Library of Congress Catalog Number: 2002113326
ISBN: 0-945-999-85-2

Published by The Independent Institute, a nonprofit, nonpartisan, scholarly
research and educational organization that sponsors comprehensive studies on the
political economy of critical social and economic issues. Nothing herein should be
construed as necessarily reflecting the views of the Institute or as an attempt to aid
or hinder the passage of any bill before Congress.

The INDEPENDENT INSTITUTE

THE INDEPENDENT INSTITUTE is a non-profit, non-partisan, scholarly research and educational organization that sponsors comprehensive studies of the political economy of critical social, economic, legal, and environmental issues.

The politicization of decision-making in society has too often confined public debate to the narrow reconsideration of existing policies. Given the prevailing influence of partisan interests, little social innovation has occurred. In order to understand both the nature of and possible solutions to major public issues, The Independent Institute's program adheres to the highest standards of independent inquiry and is pursued regardless of prevailing political or social biases and conventions. The resulting studies are widely distributed as books and other publications, and are publicly debated through numerous conference and media programs.

Through this uncommon independence, depth, and clarity, The Independent Institute pushes at the frontiers of our knowledge, redefines the debate over public issues, and fosters new and effective directions for government reform.

Contents

Preface

Throughout the affluent countries of the world, the doctrine of *sustainable development* has attracted a very wide following. Almost all the governments of the developed countries pay lip service to it, and any particular intervention in public life that can be claimed to promote the objective of sustainable development is almost automatically assumed to be justified.

Given the strength of the numerous groups and bureaucracies in society that have a vested interest in sustainable development, it is not surprising that they have not felt the need to spell out the intellectual case for it. Although many vague statements of the basic objectives and beliefs of sustainable development have been made, there has been little, if any, detailed defense of these beliefs. Consequently, it has been difficult to embark on a serious debate about sustainable development. In this monograph, I try to identify the key planks in the sustainable-development platform and to subject them to critical analysis. These planks include, of course, the usual claim that the world will soon run out of nonrenewable resources—a claim that has been growing fainter as it has been increasingly falsified—and the more important recent claim that the future of the planet is being threatened by climate change. But there is nothing new about this latter claim, and many powerful critiques of this part of the sustainable-development program have already been published.

At various points in this monograph—and particularly in the final chapter—I also examine the claim that sustainable development represents the moral high ground, that it represents greater respect for the rights of future generations and for the dictates of intergenerational justice. I show that this claim is without foundation. Furthermore, I argue that the sustainable development lobby's strange obsession with future supplies of material resources—in spite of its proclaimed disdain for mere material possessions—only diverts attention from the most important persistent threat to human welfare. This threat is one that is not automatically dispelled by the economic growth that can be expected to take place over the course of the twenty-first century: the ever-present threat to democratic liberties, involving the widespread violation of human rights throughout much of the world. My conclusion is that the most important bequest we can make to future generations is a world in which there is greater respect for human rights and liberties than is the case today. The only development that is sustainable now is development that enables people to live together peacefully.

Finally, I would to thank Oxford University Press for permission to draw on some material previously published in my book *Justice, Posterity, and the Environment* co-authored with Joanna Pasek, and in my contribution to *Fairness and Futurity*, edited by A. Dobson. I also thank Edward Elgar for permission to use material in *Economic Growth and Valuation of the Environment* edited by Ekko van Ierland, and the editors of the journal *Environmental Values*. I am also greatly indebted to Alexander Tabarrok of The Independent Institute for major and valuable comments on an earlier draft and to anonymous referees for useful comments on a later draft.

Introduction

During the last few years, the politically correct slogan that has swept the developed world and that has been the foundation for a great expansion of bureaucratic activity at both the national and the international level is *sustainable development*. Together with the so-called *precautionary principle,* the sustainable-development slogan is widely presented as a great new insight that should be used to guide policy.

The object of this monograph is to show that the support for sustainable development is based on a confusion about its ethical implications and on a flagrant disregard of the relevant factual evidence. Indeed, the popularity of sustainable development cannot be explained by reference to its intellectual coherence, for it is founded on two indefensible propositions. The first is the positive proposition that economic growth will soon come up against the limits of resource availability. It is argued that action is required to reduce to "sustainable" levels the rate at which resources are used—an impossible task, of course, unless we were to stop using some resources completely. In chapters 2 and 3, I show the predictions of imminent exhaustion of resources to be unfounded, both on theoretical grounds and in the light of a mass of evidence. The true prospects for economic growth over the course of this century are that future generations will be much richer than people alive today.

In chapters 4 and 5 I go on to show that one particular major current fear is greatly exaggerated: namely, that the growth—indeed the survival—of the human race is at risk from the danger of climate change. So although the climate-change problem has to be taken seriously and the results of scientific research into this problem over the coming years have to be followed closely, there is no case for any drastic action now, in the present state of knowledge and given the many other urgent problems facing us, to combat climate change. Nor is this conclusion invalidated by the appeal to the precautionary principle.

The second fundamental principle underlying the campaigns for sustainable development is that it represents the moral high ground. Apparently, it does so largely because it places more emphasis on intergenerational equity than do conventional economic principles. In chapter 7, I seek to demonstrate that this part of the case for sustainable development is also flawed. In fact, coherent reasons are rarely given for believing that sustainable development is an ethically superior goal to the conventional economists' goal of maximizing the sum of human welfare over future generations, and vague hand-waving in the direction of intergenerational justice or equity or the rights of future generations is apparently assumed to be enough to shame any critics of sustainable development. But if these concepts are examined more closely, as I do in chapter 7, it transpires that they have little or no relevance to the problem of how we ought to conceive our obligations to future generations.

If, therefore, the increasing popularity of the concept of sustainable development cannot be explained by its intellectual strength, its growing influence on international and national policy might perhaps be better explained by reference to sociological phenomena, such as the public's appetite for dramatic environmental scare stories or politicians' tendency to jump on media-supported bandwagons. Such phenomena also fit easily into what economists describe as the rent-seeking behavior of various agents in society: each agent seeks to maximize its market power by means other than socially valuable methods of increasing productive efficiency and the like.[1] Thus, the popularity of sustainable development might be explained by the combined power of numerous bodies that can successfully exploit some of the sociological phenomena mentioned above in order to expand their power.

Such bodies include enterprises that hope to gain from subsidies to the manufacture of, say, low-carbon forms of energy such as fuel cells, methanol, wind turbines, and the like; bureaucrats who want to expand their budgets and get promotions by showing how many more projects they need to direct and how many more regulations they have to apply; the media, who can find bigger markets if they pander to the public's appetite for stories that tell them that we are all living on the edge of an exciting precipice instead of leading rather boring and monotonous lives; and environmentalist pressure groups eager to expand their memberships and budgets. Backed up by politicians who can recognize a good bandwagon when they see one, this coalition of forces is certain to win—at least in rich countries. Everybody can join. Any pet project—ranging from dislike of traffic congestion and concern for the bald eagle to fear that our grandchildren will be deprived of essential materials for survival—can qualify for inclusion under the sustainable development banner. No scientific proof or serious logical argument is necessary to gain support for any particular cause. All that is needed to ensure that one's pet project or preference wins approval is to chant the mantra "this is needed in the interests of sustainable development" or to refer knowingly to the dictates of the mysterious precautionary principle.

1

What Is *Sustainable Development* Supposed to Mean?

Sustainable Development and Conceptual Chaos

The first question that has to be asked about sustainable development is, What exactly does it mean? The second question is, What is so good about it? This chapter focuses on the first question.

One of the most famous definitions of sustainable development is that contained in the Brundtland Report, *Our Common Future*: "development that meets the needs of the present without compromising the ability of future generations to meet their own needs" (World Commission on Environment and Development [WCED] 1987: 43).[2] But such a criterion is not very helpful. Not every need of the present generation is being met, so why should future generations be any different? Moreover, people at different points in time or at different income levels or with different cultural or national backgrounds differ about the importance they attach to different needs. The injunction that we should enable future generations to meet their needs does not provide any clear guidance as to what has to be preserved in order that future generations may do so.

Furthermore, this injunction seems to leave no room for trade-offs. Suppose we accept the claim of some environmental activists that future generations will face more serious environmental problems than those we currently face. How many of the needs (and wants, if such things differ) of the current generation are to be sacrificed in order to help future generations meet their needs? The urgency of needs varies enormously, even for a given individual, let alone for different individuals and then different generations. The term *needs* does not stand for some objective,

1

homogeneous, and indivisible entity. So no guidance is provided by the statement that the ability of the present generation to meet its needs must not be sacrificed at all in order to enable future generations to meet their needs.

The Brundtland Report also contains another concept of sustainable development that is not so much meaningless as morally outrageous. The report states that "The loss of plant and animal species can greatly limit the options of future generations; so sustainable development requires the conservation of plant and animal species" (WCED 1987: 43). But, we might ask, how far does the Brundtland Report's injunction really go? What price must we pay to conserve all plant and animal species for posterity? Are we supposed to mount a large operation, at astronomic cost, to ensure the survival of every known and unknown species on the grounds that they may give pleasure to future generations or may turn out, in a hundred years' time, to have medicinal properties? Approximately 98 percent of all the species that have ever existed are believed to have become extinct already, but most people do not suffer any great sense of loss as a result. How many people lose sleep because it is no longer possible to see a live dinosaur?

Clearly, absolutist conceptions of sustainable development—for example, that we have to maintain the environment exactly as it is today—are morally repugnant. Given the acute poverty and environmental degradation in which many of the world's population live, we cannot justify using up vast resources in an attempt to save from extinction, say, every single one of the several million species of beetle that exist. Resources would be better devoted to more urgent environmental concerns, such as increasing access to clean drinking water or sanitation in the Third World or raising educational standards for females in some developing countries where a major obstacle to raising living standards is a high birth rate.

When it soon became obvious that the "strong" concept of sustainable development was morally indefensible, as well as totally impracticable, many environmentalists shifted their ground. A new version was adopted, known in the literature as "weak" sustainability. This version of sustainability allows for some natural resources to be run down as long as adequate compensation is provided by increases in other resources, perhaps even in the form of man-made capital. But what constitutes adequate compensation? How many more schools or hospitals or houses or factories or machines are required to compensate for using up some mineral resources or forests or clean atmosphere? The answer, it turned out, is that the acceptability of the substitution is to be judged by its contribution to sustaining human welfare.

For example, John Pezzey, in an authoritative and extensive survey, concludes that most definitions still "understand sustainability to mean sustaining an improvement (or at least maintenance) in the quality of life, rather than just sustaining the existence of life" (1992: 11). He went on to adopt as a "standard definition of sustainable development" one according to which welfare per head of population must never decline (ibid).[3] The same definition is adopted in the editorial introduction to a more recent extensive collection of articles on sustainable development, where it is stated that "non-negative change in economic welfare per capita becomes the intertemporal equity objective" (Faucheux, Pearce, and Proops, 1996: 4). This definition has also been confirmed in other authoritative sources.[4]

One important feature of these definitions is that they are couched in terms of maintaining well-being or welfare, not some concept such as the overall stock of natural capital. In other words, they allow for substitutability between natural and man-made capital provided that, on balance, there is no decline in welfare. The central variable, welfare, that must not be allowed to decline is thus treated as some sort of catchall variable. But if the choice between preserving natural capital and adding to, or preserving, man-made capital depends on which of them makes the greater contribution to welfare, the whole point of replacing the orthodox economist's paradigm of welfare maximization with some allegedly wider concept that incorporates non-welfarist values is fatally undermined. In the attempt to rid the original "strong" concept of sustainable development of its most obvious weaknesses, the baby has been thrown out with the bathwater.

In addition to the appeal that conventional economic growth is unsustainable or unethical, a third line of argument in favor of sustainable development is often deployed. This argument abandons any attempt to provide a precise definition of sustainable development and offers instead a ragbag of all sorts of desirable objectives in whatever field of human activity one likes to imagine. For example, in the United States the Clinton administration set up the President's Council on Sustainable Development in 1993 and an Interagency Working Group on Sustainable Development in 1996 to oversee implementation of the council's recommendations. In its turn, the working group created three task forces. The first of these task forces set out in detail the main objectives of sustainable development, which include items such as increased per capita income and employment, decreased violent crime, decreased traffic congestion, and a host of other worthy objectives, none of which seems to have any connection with the idea of sustainable development.

Similarly, in the introduction to a recent survey of policies on sustainable development, the authors suggest that, for their purposes: "it is not necessary to adjudicate among slightly different presentations of the core principles of sustainable development. In our view, it is sufficient to note that . . . sustainable development indicates an interdependent concern with: promoting human welfare; satisfying basic needs; protecting the environment; considering the fate of future generations; achieving equity between rich and poor; and participating on a broad basis in development decision-making. While these points may appear vague, they are not without content" (Lafferty and Meadowcroft 2000: 19).

Just these two illustrations—it is too easy to cite many others—demonstrate the way that sustainable development has become an all-embracing concept to the extent that it has no clear analytical bite at all. It is true that—as the great British economist Arthur Pigou spelled out clearly several decades ago—economic welfare is not the whole of welfare. It is merely that part of it that can, in his famous phrase, "be brought directly or indirectly into relation with the measuring rod of money" (1932: 11). It is right that one should also be concerned with other ingredients of the quality of life, such as personal and social relationships or certain aspects of the environment that may not be commensurate with economic welfare. But almost everybody would be in favor of measures to help improve such aspects of human welfare. Only criminals would oppose a reduction in violent crime. The whole problem is the selection of the means toward these ends and the assessment of trade-offs of one against the other. Here the concept of sustainable development has nothing to add. Indeed, it subtracts from the objective of maximization of human welfare because the slogan of sustainable development seems to provide a blanket justification for almost any policy designed to promote almost any ingredient of human welfare irrespective of its cost and hence irrespective of the sacrifice of other ingredients of welfare.

The Measurement of Sustainable Development

The impossibility of devising an intellectually coherent and operational definition of sustainable development is illustrated by the difficulties faced by bodies that have attempted to measure sustainability. For example, at the United Nations Conference on Environment and Development (UNCED) in Rio de Janeiro, the United Kingdom committed itself to develop a set of indicators to show whether Britain's development was becoming more sustainable (Department of the Environment [DOE] 1996: 1). As part of this effort, an interdepartmental working group was set up (of course) to consider the matter and report on its findings. Few bureaucrats are likely to dispute the necessity for such a group because for many people committees are places where conversation is a substitute for the boredom of work and the loneliness of thought. Unfortunately, as the working group's report concedes, it is not at all clear what sustainable development means, so it is difficult to know how to measure it or which policies promote it (UK DOE 1996: 5).

Very recently (January 2001) an important attempt was made to introduce some intellectually respectable measurement into the sustainability literature: an *environmental sustainability index* (ESI) for 122 countries, produced by a team under the direction of Dan Esty of Yale University and involving the collaboration of teams at Yale and Columbia Universities (Esty et al. 2001).[5] This index is undoubtedly the most serious, original, and thoughtful contribution to the debate produced so far. Its statistical analyses are highly professional (notwithstanding what seems to be a mysterious elementary arithmetical mistake).[6] It clearly represents a major research effort to bring together a new and extensive range of environmental data, and it is very honest both about gaps in the data and about the methodology. The study was also supported by private funds, not by the taxpayer.

Unfortunately, the index fails to come to grips with the sustainability part of the concept of environmental sustainability. It is claimed that

> environmental sustainability can be presented as a function of five phenomena: (1) the state of the environmental *systems,* such as air, soil, ecosystems, and water; (2) the stresses on those systems, in the form of pollution and exploitation levels; (3) the *human* vulnerability to environmental change in the form of loss of food resources or exposure to environmental diseases; (4) the *social and institutional* capacity to cope with environmental challenges; and finally (5) the ability to respond to the demands of *global stewardship* by cooperating in collective efforts to conserve international environmental resources such as the atmosphere. We define environmental sustainability as the ability to produce high levels of performance on each of these dimensions in a lasting manner. We refer to these five dimensions as the core "components" of environmental sustainability. (Esty 2001: 9, italics in original.)

But the report also says that "The Index creates a series of comparative benchmarks of environmental *conditions* in different countries" (2001: 9). So apparently it is not really an index of environmental *sustainability* after all. For example, it includes measurements of urban sulfur dioxide (SO_2) and nitrogen oxide (NO_x) concentrations, and many other stock variables that are clearly indicators of environmental *conditions*. No explanation is given of why and how they are proxy variables for environmental *sustainability*. Environmental conditions in, say, late-nineteenth-century British and American cities were awful, but the cities remained standing and now generally enjoy far better environments than do most cities in poorer developing countries.

Furthermore, the index lacks any firm conceptual basis for aggregating together the constituent items of whatever it is that it is really trying to measure. The aggregation method used in the study is to group the basic sixty-seven variables that are believed to be related to environmental sustainability into twenty-two core indicators. Within each of these twenty-two groups, the underlying variables are given equal weight—that is, they are simply averaged. And then each of the twenty-two core indicators is given equal weight in arriving at the overall ESI (Esty 2001: 23).[7] Thus, a variable that is used together with three others to construct some core indicator will have only half the weight of a variable that is used, in conjunction with only one other variable to construct some other core indicator. It is not obvious that there can be any conceptual basis for this discrimination. Nor is there any explicit attempt to weigh either the underlying sixty-seven variables or the twenty-two core indicators in terms of their marginal contribution to what the index is supposed to be measuring—namely, environmental sustainability. Indeed, without some independently defined concept of environmental sustainability—that is, other than what it is that the index measures—it is difficult to see how any such weighting can be carried out.

In short, one cannot measure environmental sustainability—let alone sustainable development—just by combining together in a largely arbitrary manner a collection of what environmental indicators one can put together, basically because there is no clear conceptual basis for sustainable development to begin with.

2

Finite Resources and the Prospects for Economic Growth

Finite Resources and the Market Mechanism

As indicated above, there are two basic features of the claim that society ought to follow the path of sustainable development. One is the positive proposition that resources are finite in some meaningful sense, and the other is the normative proposition that this limitation imposes special obligations on us to respect the rights of future generations and the accompanying obligations of intergenerational justice. In this chapter and the following two chapters, I concentrate on the former.

Resources are either finite, or they are not. If they are, then the only way to ensure that they last forever is to stop using them. Bringing future economic growth to a halt is not enough. Levels of consumption need to be reduced to infinitesimal levels if finite resources are to be made to last. But, of course, even the most fanatical proponents of sustainability would hardly go that far and would soon sell a critical pass by confessing that, perhaps, after due reflection, with everything taken into account, etc., etc., etc., the human race will eventually find ways of coping with the changes that take place in the balance between demand and supply of resources.

In other words, one cannot have it both ways. Either resources are finite in some relevant sense, in which case even zero growth will fail to save us in the long run, or resources are not really finite in any relevant sense, in which case this argument for slowing down growth collapses. In a famous book published in 1972, *The Limits to Growth*, this dilemma was avoided by cutting off the computer printout at the year when it becomes clear that even a proposed stationary state will still be untenable on account of exhaustion of what was assumed to be a finite supply of resources (Meadows et al. 1972).

In fact, of course, not only are resources not finite in any relevant sense, but the evidence of all past history, including even the relatively recent past, shows that there have been no trends toward the exhaustion of any resources that matter. Similarly, past history is littered with predictions of imminent resource scarcity that have been subsequently falsified. Malthus's predictions approximately two hundred years ago—namely that world population would soon outrun food supplies—are probably the most famous. But more than two thousand years earlier Pericles in Ancient Greece made equally false similar predictions (French 1964).

More recently, various empirical studies have again and again predicted impending exhaustion of materials. For example, a study carried out in 1929 concluded that "the world's resources [of lead] cannot meet present demands." But for the rest of the twentieth century nobody worried about a lead shortage. In fact, people have been more worried that too much of it is around. The same 1929 report concluded that "the known resources of tin . . . do not seem to satisfy the ever increasing demand of the industrial nations for more than 10 years."[8] More than forty years later, the authors of *The Limits to Growth* (Meadows et al. 1972) were worried because existing "known" reserves of tin were only enough to last for another fifteen years. Still, that expectation was better than the 1929 prediction that the reserves were supposed to last us for only ten years. At this rate, we shall have to wait millions of years before we have identified enough tin reserves to last us forever. Meanwhile we shall just have to go on using up that ten years' supply that was all we were believed to have back in 1929.

Soon after the Second World War, the famous Paley report was prepared in response to a fear in the United States about increasing scarcity of domestic mineral supplies. This report confirmed that domestic supplies would be inadequate, so that rising demand for increasingly scarce imported supplies would raise their prices in relation to the prices of manufactured goods and move the terms of trade against the industrial nations of the world. In the end, of course, nothing of the sort has happened; indeed, much of the aid received by Third World countries has been offset by a deterioration in their terms of trade.

There are two main reasons why past predictions of imminent exhaustion of minerals have proved wrong. First, they are invariably based on comparisons between existing known reserves of most mineral resources and the rate at which they are being used up, indicating a misunderstanding of the meaning of reserves statistics. Second, they ignore the economic mechanisms that are set in motion when any resource becomes scarce.

As regards the former point, the usual estimates of known reserves of raw materials (namely, those published by the U.S. Bureau of Mines) are conservative contingency forecasts made by the exploration companies, and *they are related to a certain price and the existing state of technical knowledge:* if the price is higher, more resources can be exploited commercially. In other words, the known reserves represent the reserves that have been worth finding, given the price and the prospects of demand and the costs of exploration. The existence of only fifty years' supply of material X at current rates of utilization is no cause for concern for the simple reason that there is rarely any point in companies' employing geologists to prospect for supplies to last humankind to the end of eternity. For example, is it seriously imagined that if there were already one thousand years of known and economically exploitable reserves of copper, any geologist would be employed in looking for new copper supplies?

And it is no answer to say that those of us who refuse to be alarmed have "overlooked" the fact that growth is faster than in the past or that world demand is on a much higher level altogether, or to bandy about some other such vague adjective. The same could have been said at almost any time in the past without being followed by exhaustion of supplies. For example, during the nineteenth century copper consumption rose approximately fortyfold, and around the turn of the century demand for copper was accelerating from an annual average growth rate of approximately 3.3 percent per annum, taking the average of the nineteenth century as a whole, to approximately 6.4 percent per annum during the period 1890 to 1910. Annual consumption had been approximately 16,000 tons in the first decade of the nineteenth century and was more than 700,000 tons in the first decade of the twentieth century. Given this rapid growth of consumption, the known reserves of copper at almost any time in the nineteenth century would have been exhausted many times over by subsequent consumption if there had been no new discoveries. But at the end of the nineteenth century known reserves were greater than at the beginning.[9]

The Recent History

Even in the postwar world, with what are believed to be unprecedented rates of economic growth, the story is the same. Indeed, one of the reasons for faster rates of economic growth has been faster development of basic resources. Thus, resources have *more than* increased to match demand. For example, in 1945, estimated known copper reserves were 100 million metric tons. During the following twenty-five years of *unprecedented* growth, 93 million metric tons were mined, so if one were to accept the ecodoomsters' analysis, there should have been almost no copper left by the end of the period. But no, reserves were estimated at more than 300 million tons—three times what they were at the outset. The same applied to zinc: known reserves of zinc were only 63 million tons in 1949, so all of it should have been used up given that production of zinc during the fast-growth years up to 1970 amounted to 75 million tons. In fact, reserves in 1970 were 123 million tons. Similarly, iron ore reserves rose fivefold during the 1960s, and bauxite reserves rose sevenfold in the fast-growing 1950s and 1960s.

The same story was repeated in later years, as can be seen in table 1. For a number of the key minerals that were the basis for the predictions of impending exhaustion of resources in the *Limits to Growth* report, the reserves thirty years later were far greater—in some cases a multiple—than those shown in that report in 1970. But the interesting point is that in the intervening thirty years consumption of all the minerals in question had been substantial and, in some cases, had even exceeded the initial estimates of known reserves! In other words, by some miracle (known to most of us as *market forces*) the world had consumed more resources than it

TABLE 1
Reserves and Consumption of Key Minerals, 1970 and 1999.

Product	Estimated reserves (million metric tons)		Cumulative consumption (million metric tons, approx.) 1970–1999
	1970	mid-1999	
Aluminium	1,170	34,000	430
Copper	308	650	290
Lead	91	140	150
Nickel	67	140	22
Zinc	123	430	190

Note: 1970 reserve estimates are from Meadows et al. 1972: 56–58. 1999 reserves estimates include "demonstrated reserves that are currently economic or marginally economic plus some that are currently sub-economic" (*World Almanac* 2000: 31, taken from the U.S. Geological Survey and the U.S. Department of the Interior). The figures of aluminium reserves include bauxite expressed as aluminium equivalent. Consumption estimates are from *Materials Bulletin's Prices and Data*, annual (Surrey, UK: Metal Bulletin Books Ltd.).

thought it had possessed and yet finished up with more than the amount with which it had started. The same applies to fuel reserves, which are discussed more fully in the next chapter.

In short, the main reason why we will never run out of any resource or even suffer seriously from any sudden reduction in its supply is that whenever demand for any particular material begins to run up against supply limitations, a wide variety of economic forces are set in motion to remedy the situation. These forces start with a rise in price, which, in turn leads to all sorts of secondary favorable feedbacks—notably a shift to substitutes, an increase in exploration, and technical progress that brings down the costs of exploration and refining and processing as well as the costs of the substitutes. In the longer run, of course, the relative prices of some of the materials in question may still rise, which will cause demand for them to contract gradually toward more and more highly valued uses. If, for example, coal were ever to become a very scarce commodity, its price would rise to the point where, like other scarce minerals such as diamonds, it would be used only for jewelry or certain very special industrial applications. We would never run out of it. And the process would take place very gradually, allowing time for economies to adapt. Key materials disappear overnight only in science fiction stories. Meanwhile, in the short run, a growing shortage of any one product will stimulate recourse to substitutes.

So the real issue is how much is economic growth likely to be constrained in the foreseeable future by increased scarcity of some input into the chain of production. This is an empirical issue, and I have set out the reasons for believing that economic growth is in no danger of coming to an end because of resource constraints. Society adapts all the time to changes in demand and supply. Even if, in spite of an astronomic rise in its price, some resource did finally run out, society will by that time have learned to live with almost no consumption of it. As I have said elsewhere and will no doubt repeat, modern civilization has survived without any supplies at all of Beckermonium, the product named after my grandfather, who failed to discover it in the nineteenth century.

The Case of Food

Under normal conditions, output of food responds to market conditions in the same way that the output of other goods responds. As population has grown, food supplies have increased more than proportionately so that world food per capita is higher now than ever before and food prices are lower. In the short run, however, an increase in demand or more likely a fall in supply can increase price so much that poor people starve. The great famines of the twentieth century, however, were caused not by failures of supply to keep up with demand but by civil wars or appalling government policies, such as the collectivization policies carried out by Stalin in the prewar period and China's "Great Leap Forward" after World War II (see, in particular, Drèze and Sen 1989 and 1990; Sen 1994).

But none of the facts about the long-run decline in food prices or the way that the growth of food has consistently outstripped the growth of world population seems to make any impact on the alarmists. A recent survey of scare stories reminds us of Paul Ehrlich's statement in the early 1970s that "The battle to feed humanity is over. In the 1970s the world will undergo famines— hundreds of millions of people are going to starve to death."[10] Similarly, in 1974 Ehrlich forecast a "nutritional disaster that seems likely to overtake humanity in the 1970s (or, at the latest, the 1980s) . . . before 1985 mankind will enter a genuine age of scarcity" in which "the accessible supplies of many key minerals will be nearing depletion" (Ehrlich and Ehrlich 1974).[11]

The survey goes on to point out that "He [Ehrlich] was not alone. Lester Brown of the Worldwatch Institute began predicting in 1973 that population would soon outstrip food production, and he still does so every time there is a temporary increase in wheat prices. In 1994, after 21 years of being wrong, he said 'After 40 years of record food production gains, output per person has reversed with unanticipated abruptness.' Two bumper harvests followed and the price of wheat fell to record lows. Yet Mr. Brown's pessimism remains as impregnable to facts as his views are popular with news-papers." The same survey gives other predictions that have been fal-sified equally dramatically, but such falsification never seems to shake the faith of their authors or to lessen the extent to which the media and public figures who ought to know better continue to take their predictions seriously.

By contrast with the continually falsified predictions of imminent worldwide food shortage the reality is that "On practically every count, humankind is now *better* nourished. The Green Revolution has been victorious. Production in the developing countries has tripled. The calorie intake per capita has here increased by 38 per-cent." (Lomborg, 2001: 67). And, as Lomborg has effectively demonstrated on the basis of unimpeachable studies by the United Nations Food and Agriculture Organization and the United Nations Environment Program, the oft-repeated assertion that the increase in world per capita food production during the last few decades has been obtained at the cost of massive soil erosion, thereby storing up obstacles to future increases, is totally unfounded. (Lomborg, 2001: 104-6). Of course, there are still major pockets of hunger in some parts of the world, notably Africa. But these are far more the result of political developments than of any technological limitations on the potential to supply food for the inhabitants.

How Much Richer Are Future Generations Likely to Be?

All long-range predictions of economic growth rates are hazardous. How many people, for example, would have predicted in the 1980s that the Japanese economy was soon to enter into a period of prolonged economic stagnation? But if we are predicting over very long periods, we can abstract from possible short- to medium-term forces, such as the catching-up on wartime dislocation that characterized the 1950s in many Western countries, or the recuperation from the oil shocks that characterized the 1970s, or the eccentric bursts of dogmatic monetarism that characterized the 1980s, or the speculative excesses and financial profligacy in some parts of the world that marked the later 1990s. In the very long run, these forces can be seen to be relatively transient. To predict growth rates over the next century one can appraise the fundamental determinants of economic growth. Such an appraisal suggests that the world per capita growth rate of national income, in real terms (i.e., adjusted for inflation), over the next one hundred years is likely to be somewhere between 1 and 2 percent per annum, but could be higher.

The average growth rate of real income per head in the world over the past forty years—which cover periods of exceptional growth and exceptional stagnation—has been 2.1 percent per annum (Maddison 1995).[12] And there are two reasons to believe that the future growth rate is likely to be at least as high, if not higher. First, in the long run, the main sources of growth in income per head are technological and scientific progress and the rate at which the resulting inventions and innovations are diffused. In turn, these depend on variables all of which are tending to increase, some at a phenomenal rate. In particular, the number of highly educated people in the world, especially those having technological and scientific qualifications, is increasing so rapidly that it far surpasses the corresponding number of people having similar qualifications only two or three decades ago, and it is likely to go on expanding rapidly. The main source of current high levels of income and output in the modern world is not so much physical capital or material resources but human capital—that is, knowledge, training, skills, and attitudes. And there is no physical limitation on the growth of this human capital.

Second, the rate of international diffusion of innovation and technical progress—which many studies have shown to be decisive in determining growth rates—will continue to accelerate.[13] As Gore Vidal puts it, "Thanks to modern technology . . . history now comes equipped with its fast-forward button."[14] This acceleration is owing in part to the information revolution and in part to the increasing globalization of economic activity. Such speed does, of course, bring with it certain problems, but it also means that the technical progress and innovations in one country will spread more quickly than in the past, as already seems to have been the case. This rapid technological progress will be intensified by one of the more favorable aspects of the policy revolution of the 1980s, namely the widespread conversion to freer and more competitive markets (including the labor market) than had been the case previously.

The underlying forces for *long-run* growth suggest that the average annual long-run growth of output per head over the next century should be above that of the past forty years. Because this growth of output per head has been 2.1 percent, a projection of between 1 and 2 percent per annum seems on the cautious side and might be giving excessive weight to the slowing down during the last decade or so. But to simplify the argument let us assume a single figure of 1.5 percent as the annual average growth rate of real incomes per head over the next one hundred years. The power of compound interest being what it is, world average real incomes per head in the year 2100 should be 4.43 times as high as they are now!

And it should not be thought that the above guess at the annual average growth rate of gross world product (GWP) over the next one hundred years is a fanciful figure. A recent draft report of the United Nations Intergovernmental Panel on Climate Change (IPCC) adopted, for purposes of estimating possible levels of energy use and carbon emissions, four possible "story lines" (to use their terminology describing possible scenarios of rates of growth of population and incomes). These story lines put per capita GWP in one hundred years' time at between 4.3 and 20 times as high as it is today! In other words, my guesstimate is at the bottom of the range adopted by the IPCC.

And the higher IPCC scenarios themselves are by no means fanciful. As one of the contributors to the work of the IPCC points out, a tenfold rise in world incomes over the course of the projected century is consistent with per capita incomes in the rich countries rising at only 1 percent per annum and those in the developing countries rising at only 3 percent per annum.[15] The former figure is well below its long-run historical rate this century and very low considering the positive influences on economic growth set out above. Given the scope for "catching up" among developing countries, the latter figure corresponds only to their having reached by the year 2100 merely the average income level enjoyed in the rich countries today. And given the international transmission of technical knowledge and productive techniques, it is virtually inconceivable that—taken as a whole—they will have failed to achieve this level.

In short, before asking present generations—including the poorer members—to make sacrifices in the interests of future generations, one should take account of the strong likelihood that the latter will be far richer than the former. No moral credit can be earned by redistributing from the poor to the rich.

3

Energy and Biodiversity

The Income-Energy Relationship

One of the most persistent and widely publicized reasons given for the impossibility of continued economic growth is the prediction that the world will soon come up against limited supplies of sources of energy. This fear that the world is running out of energy sources is based on two kinds of data. One is the comparison between known reserves and current rates of consumption, which, as I have shown previously, is a flawed methodology. The other is a cross-country comparison of levels of income and of energy use, such as that shown in table 2.

Table 2 shows energy consumption in a selection of countries with vastly different levels of income. Such comparative data on energy (or on any other material) have been the basis for the frequently encountered argument that the poorer countries cannot aspire ever to reach the income levels currently enjoyed by the rich countries today because there are not enough resources, including energy, available. It is obvious that there must be a flaw in this argument because similar propositions about almost any other resource would have been considered equally true at any time in human history, without growth having ever been brought to a permanent halt.

But such comparative data demonstrate only that it is impossible for the poorer countries in the world to attain *immediately* the income levels currently enjoyed by the richer countries—that is, *given the total resources available today*. To interpret the data as implying that the growth of incomes over time is inevitably constrained by energy ignores the *supply* side of the income-energy relationship.

TABLE 2

*Per Capita Incomes and (Commercial) Energy Consumption
in Selected Countries and Groups of Countries.*

Country	Income (U.S. $ 1995)	Primary Energy (kg. 1994)
India	340	248
China	620	664
Egypt	790	600
Brazil	3,640	718
Argentina	8,030	1,504
Italy	19,020	2,707
United States	26,980	7,819
Low-income countries	430	369
Lower-middle-income countries	1,670	1,449
Upper-middle-income countries	4,260	1,544
High-income countries	24,930	5,066
Total world	**4,880**	**1,433**

Source: World Bank 1997: 214, table 1, and 228, table 8. The income figures refer to gross national product (GNP) per head in 1995, and the energy figures refer to commercial consumption in kilograms of oil equivalent of primary energy used, excluding firewood, dried animal excrement, and other traditional fuels.

Increased use of energy over time is not simply the result of an exogenous rise in world incomes leading to an increase in the demand for energy. Over time the total supply of usable energy has increased dramatically, and the direction of causality in the incomes-energy relationship has largely been the other way round. The rapid acceleration of economic activity during the last two centuries has been largely the result of the energy revolution—both in techniques of harnessing energy and in the discovery and exploitation of new forms of energy, in particular the transformation of primary energy into electricity.

Even for oil, which many people believe to be the primary energy source that is most limited in supply, the flaws in the usual pessimistic methodology of comparing current or predicted rates of consumption with known or estimated reserves have been evident for decades. For example, in 1950, annual world oil consumption was running at approximately 4 billion barrels per year, and proven reserves were approximately 90 billion barrels—only enough for perhaps twenty-two years' supply. But, in the subsequent forty-three years, actual consumption was more than 640 billion barrels. Furthermore, at the end of those years, proven reserves were ten times greater than they had been at the outset.[16]

Past Predictions of Energy Shortages

The falsification of predictions of rapidly approaching energy shortages—like that of materials in general—has a very distinguished pedigree. For example, back in 1865 the great economist W. S. Jevons predicted shortages of coal supplies. But, although coal demand has since increased far more than Jevons anticipated, known reserves of coal are now estimated to be enough for at least another one thousand years or so at current rates of consumption (Rogner 1997). And how many people believe that in one thousand years the world will still be using such a dirty and polluting fuel?

In spite of the decisive falsification of Jevons's predictions during the course of the subsequent decades, ninety years later the 1955 UN Atoms for Peace Conference made estimates of both proven and ultimately recoverable reserves of fossil fuels, which are now seen to be one-quarter and one-twelfth, respectively, of current estimates (Anderson 1998b: 438). One can list innumerable equally falsified predictions in later years, particularly following the 1973 oil crisis, which led the U.S. Department of Energy to predict the oil price to reach $250 a barrel by the year 2000 ("Energy Survey," *The Economist*, 10 February 2001, 13). Similarly mistaken predictions in the 1970s and later include the following:

- "Countries with expanding industry, rapid population growth . . . will be especially hard hit by economic energy scarcities from now on." (Amory Lovins in 1974)[17]
- "The supply of oil will fail to meet increasing demand before the year 2000, most probably between 1985 and 1995, even if energy prices are 50 percent above current levels in real terms." (MIT workshop in 1977)

• "The diagnosis of the U.S. energy crisis is quite simple: demand for energy is increasing, while supplies of oil and natural gas are diminishing. Unless the U.S. makes a timely adjustment before world oil becomes very scarce and very expensive in the 1980s, the nation's economic security and the American way of life will be gravely endangered." (Executive Office of the President, *National Energy Program*, in 1977)

• "The oil-based societies of the industrial world cannot be sustained and cannot be replicated. The huge increases in oil prices since 1973 virtually guarantee that the Third World will never derive most of its energy from petroleum." (Worldwatch Institute in 1979)

• "What seems certain, at least for the foreseeable future, is that energy, once cheap and plentiful but now expensive and limited, will continue to rise in cost." (Union of Concerned Scientists in 1980)

• "Conservative estimates project a price of $80 a barrel [in 1985] even if peace is restored to the Persian Gulf and an uncertain stability maintained." (*National Geographic* in 1981)

Current Estimates of Energy Resources

Of course, it may be argued that it is still too soon to claim that the pessimistic predictions will not be fulfilled even in the very long run. The above estimates of oil reserves are subject to a significant margin of uncertainty. But there are major uncertainties on the favorable side as well as on the unfavorable side. For example, some sources of oil are well known but are not currently economically and technically viable on a significant scale, but they might well become so as a result of further major cost reductions in mining and processing of these sources.[18]

The prospective supplies of other fossil fuels are also enormous, without taking account of the prospects for exploiting renewable forms of energy (which are discussed in the next section). As can be seen in table 3, reserves of natural gas amount to approximately five hundred years' consumption at current rates, and reserves of coal amount to more than a thousand years' consumption. In table 3, these three major sources of fossil fuels, converted into equivalent units (Giga tons of oil equivalent), total approximately 5,000 Gtoe, which is almost seven hundred times total world annual consumption of these three fossil fuels combined.[19]

Thus, one way or another, the assumption that energy supplies will not constitute an important constraint on the rate of economic growth in the foreseeable future seems to be fully justified. Indeed, current expert opinion is that "the availability of fossil fuel resources can be measured in units of hundreds—perhaps thousands—of years. The availability of renewable energy resources (including geothermal resources), even if used on an immensely expanded scale, has no known time limit" (Anderson 1998a: 30).

Furthermore, the figures in table 3 take no account of the scope for major improvements in (1) the economic viability of renewable energy (especially solar power), or (2) the likely continuation in the trend toward greater efficiency in the use of energy and the declining energy intensity of output in developed countries. Nor do they include geothermal energy.[20]

In regard to the continued technical progress in the use of renewable energy, the total energy received from the sun is perhaps ten thousand times the total world energy consumption, and if only a very small fraction of this solar energy could be harnessed in an economically viable manner, the energy problem would disappear. Indeed, technical progress in the harnessing of solar energy has been substantial. Already photovoltaic systems and solar-thermal

TABLE 3

Consumption Rates and Aggregate Global Resources of Fossil Fuels (Giga Tons of Oil Equivalent).

	Consumption (per annum)	*Discovered* (1994)	*Further Resources*	*Total*
Oil	3.37	333	481	814
Natural gas	1.87	333	537	870
Coal	2.16	1,003	2,397	3,400
Total	7.40	1,669	3,415	5,084

Source: Anderson 1998b: 437, referring to data in Rogner 1997. The figures for oil comprise what are known as conventional and unconventional sources, the latter including oil shales, tar sands, and coal-bed methane.

power stations, such as those now operating in California, manage to convert approximately 10 percent of the incident solar energy into electricity, and with further developments in the pipeline, are expected to be converting approximately 20 percent of solar energy in the near future. On conservative assumptions concerning the duration of sunlight and conversion efficiency, it can be shown that only approximately 0.25 percent of the area now under crops and permanent pastures would be needed to meet all of the world's primary energy demand. Even if this demand rises—as it may well do—fourfold over the course of the next century, only 1 percent of this land area will be needed to supply the world demand for energy. Costs and storage are the main constraints, not land, to meeting this demand (Anderson 1998a).[21]

But given the pace of technical progress, especially in fuel cells that can store or produce electricity, there is every reason to believe that these latter constraints will continue to be loosened. Such rapid progress is now being reported in the development of fuel cells for use in cars that automobile firms expect them to be commercially viable within a decade or two.[22] Progress is also being made in developing economically viable wind power. Although there has been legitimate opposition to the spread of wind farms in countries where space is at a premium, some experts believe that the potential for economically viable wind power in North America, the former Soviet Union, Africa, and other parts of the world is such that it might meet 20 percent or more of the world's electricity demand within the next few decades (Grubb and Meyer 1993).[23]

Indeed, it is likely that the only constraint on the pace of research and development of ways of exploiting renewable forms of energy will be a fall in the price of fossil fuels. Many local specialized uses of renewable energy are already competitive with fossil fuel-based energy. But the prices of the latter might still be reduced substantially in many parts of the world, aided in part by technological progress in discovery, extraction, and processing, not to mention the large cushion of prices over extraction costs of oil in many parts of the world. So the future is likely to be much more one of competition between renewable and nonrenewables. As technological change reduces the price of renewables, the monopoly power of fossil fuel producers will decline, leading to further long-term declines in real energy prices. Environmentalists may find it a sad irony, but for the rest of humanity one of the great benefits of lower-priced renewables could well be a fall in the price of fossil fuels.

Nor should one overlook the demand side of the energy demand-supply balance. For one major influence has been the increasing efficiency of energy use. Lomborg has documented the vast reduction in the amount of energy used per unit of output that has taken place in the largest industrial economies and the scope for yet further major improvements in energy efficiency once it becomes economically attractive. As an example of the potential, in Denmark less energy was used in 1989 than in 1970 in spite of GNP having risen by forty-eight percent over the period in question (Lomborg, 2001, 125–6).

Biodiversity

In addition to the constraints on materials—especially food and energy—that are alleged to make continued economic growth unsustainable, it is also widely asserted that economic growth is leading to mass destruction of biodiversity. This destruction, it is alleged, has two types of harmful effects. First, it deprives the human race of an essential input into our welfare, notably as a source of future medicinal remedies. Second, it is regarded to be a striking example of the way in which we are depriving future generations of the environmental inheritance that is their due. Here I consider only the former assertion.

Most of the world's biodiversity is found in tropical or semitropical regions, which happen to be mainly in developing countries. In the past, any loss of biodiversity caused by humans was the result of hunting, but in modern times it is caused almost entirely by the damage done to the habitat of millions of species that live in forests, particularly in tropical and semitropical countries.

How much deforestation is actually going on and at what rate species are being made extinct as a result are not yet amenable to anything like precise measurement. This immeasurability is not so much on account of uncertainty about the former, although the rate of this destruction is often exaggerated.[24] The main reason for our ignorance about the rate of species extinction is that we do not know (1) within an order of magnitude of ten how many species there are to begin with, or (2) the number of species becoming extinct each year. The eminent zoologist Sir (now Lord) Robert May, who, until very recently, was the chief scientific adviser to the British government and who is a foremost authority on the question, has suggested that the "best guess" one can make about the number of species in existence is approximately 7 million, though a possible range might be anywhere between 3 million and 100 million, and that some experts believe that the most plausible range is between 5 million and 15 million (May 1997: table 4).[25]

Estimates of extinctions are also inevitably very uncertain because one does not actually observe the death of what is known as the last pair of any species. Thus, the fact that only 641 species have been certified as having become extinct since the year 1600 does not exclude the possibility that many more have become extinct without our knowing about it, particularly because the vast majority of species (including plants and animals) are insects, and approximately 40 percent of these are beetles (May 2000). Estimates of species extinctions have to be based on statistical projections from scanty data. In a recent lecture, May, whose writings suggest that he is among those who are rather alarmed at the rate of species extinction, mentioned that one common method of estimating the rate of species extinction implied that species were becoming extinct, largely through the loss of tropical forests, at the rate of about 0.3 percent per annum, which would correspond to about 6 percent becoming extinct over the next twenty years (May 2000). Lomborg's survey of a number of unimpeachable sources, including the International Union for the Conservation of Nature, suggests that the rate of species extinction is far less than this. (Lomborg, 2001: 252-6).

But even May's figure is in sharp contrast to the figure proposed by Thomas Lovejoy of the Smithsonian Institution, a well-known commentator on the subject, in the BBC's Reith Lectures in 2000. He predicted (as he has been doing for decades) that a quarter or more of all species would become extinct during the next twenty years—that is, approximately four times the May guesstimate.[26] But Lovejoy's own figures do not match his prediction. Instead, they tend to confirm May's much lower estimate of the current rate of species extinction, for, according to Lovejoy, species are currently being made extinct at about 1,000 to 10,000 times the normal rate. He did not say what the normal rate was, but he is on record as accepting that the rate of species extinction from the beginning of the twentieth century to 1980 averaged approximately one species per year. So if one species per year were "normal," we should now be losing between 1,000 and 10,000 species per year.

Suppose, to simplify the arithmetic, we take a figure near the middle of this range, namely 5,000 species per year. This figure would amount to 100,000 species becoming extinct after twenty years. If we then take the midpoint of the estimated range of the number of species in existence mentioned previously (i.e., 10 million), after twenty years only 1 percent of all species would have become extinct, by comparison with Lovejoy's figure of 25 percent. Even if we take the top figure of Lovejoy's estimate of the range for extinctions (i.e., 10,000 per annum), we would still end up with a cumulative loss after twenty years of only approximately 2 percent.[27] Thus, without in any way wishing to minimize the need for concern about loss of biodiversity, I must note that many of the alarming figures bandied about concerning rates at which species are becoming extinct—even in what was once regarded as the serious and prestigious BBC Reith Lectures series—appear to be vast exaggerations.

Indeed, one of the most alarming features of the whole debate is the unscientific attitude of some distinguished biologists. For example, Professor Ehrlich is on record as saying that "biologists don't need to know how many species there are, how they are related to one another or how many disappear annually to recognize that Earth's biota is entering a gigantic spasm of extinction" (quoted in Lomborg, 2001: 254).

But whatever the facts about the rate of loss of biodiversity, the question here is how far it is the result of market failures of one kind or another. In many of these tropical and semitropical countries, rapidly expanding populations and absence of alternative employment opportunities is in part or in whole responsible for the destruction of forests. Deforestation is also sometimes caused by multinational companies engaged in building roads and in logging or mining operations. In these operations, they destroy the habitat of the species living in the forests without taking into account the possible potential value of the species in question to the world as a whole. Such companies may have little or no stake in the long-term sustainability of the environmental assets in question.

But deforestation is also often the result of market distortions caused by the domestic policies of the countries in which the biodiversity loss is experienced. Such policies may include the absence of clearly designed property rights (with inadequate protection of the rights of indigenous people in the areas concerned) so that poor farmers have no incentive to husband deforested areas in a sustainable manner, as well as subsidies and tax breaks that encourage excessive transformation of forests into other uses. And in some countries, government regulations designed to curtail logging are simply flouted or evaded on a massive scale.[28]

Unequal bargaining power of the parties involved might also sometimes mean that even though rapid deforestation may confer short-run economic advantages on the developing countries in question or on some multinational corporations, the longer-run effects may be very harmful to the local economies and communities. How far is there also a longer-term loss for the world as a whole?

One of the most widely held arguments for believing that a loss of biodiversity is harmful for the whole of the human race is that the loss of certain species of plants may deprive the world as a whole (and future generations) of some medicinal benefits that might otherwise have been obtained from them. If the continued existence of these plants is believed to be potentially valuable to the whole human race, then their destruction in country X harms other countries, if not now, then in the future; that is, it is an example of what economists call a *negative externality.* It is widely believed that tropical rainforests are full of potential drug material, but it is not clear how important this potential benefit may be compared to the progress in medical science that can be made by laboratory research and development. For example, between 1960 and 1982 the National Cancer Institute in the United States and the U.S. Department of Agriculture examined and tested approximately 35,000 samples of roots, fruits, and bark from 12,000 species of plants. Only three of them were found to be of any significance. And, of course, large pharmaceutical companies have not been blind to the possibility that some of the species in tropical areas may have medicinal value. Indeed, some of them have long been carrying out major projects to screen species for this purpose.

But the potential pharmaceutical value of plants in tropical forests tends to be exaggerated on account of a failure to deduct the costs involved in screening, developing, producing, and marketing successful drugs (Mendelsohn and Balick, 1995). This is largely because the success rate in identifying useful plants has been very low, and some pharmaceutical companies have been cutting down on these activities in favor of more laboratory research designed, essentially, with the same end purpose in mind: namely, to identify the characteristics of substances—whether natural or synthetic—that have potential medicinal benefits. For example, Shaman Pharmaceuticals, which was the leading proponent of the so-called ethnobotanical approach to drug discovery, sent teams of physicians and botanists into the rainforests of Asia, Africa, and South America, where they collaborated with local healers in identifying plants with medicinal properties. But the results were very meager and the company has now gone bankrupt. Merck, one of the world's largest drug companies, spent ten years trying to extract and develop the active principles from Chinese herbal remedies without success. Other firms too are scaling down their activities in this area in favor of methods for screening the vast numbers of artificial products that have now been created by modern combinatorial chemistry.[29]

But although pharmaceutical companies are probably well equipped to estimate the relative private payoff to research into species of potential medicinal value, it may well be that, from the social point of view, they are not doing enough of this research. For example, their private net revenue will include a deduction for their tax payments, which are not a social cost, of course. Also the drugs will continue to have a social value after the patent rights have been exhausted and the attached monopoly profits come to an end. On the other hand, some newly discovered drugs may really represent superior alternatives to established drugs, so that the *net* gain to society will be less than the value of the new drugs taken in isolation. For one reason or another, therefore, there may be a case for subsidizing the researches of pharmaceutical companies in this area. But it should be born in mind that research in general is already subsidized so it needs to be demonstrated that additional specific subsidies are needed to protect biodiversity. Given the exaggerated assertions about the rate of deforestation and of the value to society of undiscovered medicinally useful plants, there is certainly no presumption that slowing down economic growth will help or that drastic action is needed to preserve tropical forests.

Conclusion

There is no empirical basis for the fear that continued economic growth is unsustainable. Past predictions that economic growth would soon come to a halt have been shown to be based on seriously flawed methods. Not surprisingly, therefore, they have been decisively refuted by events. Even with respect to food or energy supplies—two types of resource that have been most frequently the subject of pessimistic predictions—there is no cause for alarm. Another allegedly disastrous consequence of economic growth, namely the destruction of biodiversity, also appears to be exaggerated, although government subsidies and a failure to enforce property rights have led to an excessive rate of deforestation in some countries and it may well be that the social value of research into the potential medicinal value of plants in tropical forests exceeds the private return to pharmaceutical companies. But these are market failures that imply a misallocation of resources *at any given point in time*. Optimal growth policy, however, is a matter of the allocation of resources *over time*. Furthermore, slower growth is much more likely to perpetuate market failures than to promote their elimination. For faster economic growth makes it easier to compensate those who may lose out from an elimination of market imperfections.

But supporters of sustainable development are quick to point out that the optimistic scenario sketched out above might be disrupted by climate change or some other catastrophic result of economic growth. Even if the optimistic scenario is the most likely, these critics argue that society ought to apply the so-called precautionary principle to environmental policy. In the next two chapters, therefore, I briefly consider these two lines of argument.

4

Climate Change

The Climate Change Constraint

The above assessment of future economic growth prospects are based on the assumption that there will be no disastrous environmental developments. But Green pressure groups widely claim that unchecked climate change will lead to catastrophic declines in world income. According to this view, drastic international action ought to be taken immediately to reduce carbon emissions, particularly by the advanced countries, who are regarded as being morally responsible for the existing high carbon concentrations in the atmosphere.

But three key points need to be established in order to justify international action to reduce carbon emissions on the grounds of overall benefit to the world community:

1. that predictions of significant climate change are reasonably reliable;
2. that the damage climate change might impose on the world as a whole will exceed the costs of limiting or preventing it; and
3. that the distribution of the costs and benefits among countries of actions to drastically cut carbon emissions is accepted as reasonably equitable.

But only the first link in the chain of argument gets much attention in the media, which may in part be because it is the only link that has any strength at all. And even that strength is probably exaggerated by the vast scientific and bureaucratic establishment that is financing its research and building empires and careers on the back of the threat of global warming, and that is backed up by manufacturers of nuclear power stations, renewable energy systems, energy-saving equipment, and so on, who all either are hoping to receive subsidies for their research programs or are hedging their bets in the event that measures are taken to enforce stringent reductions in carbon emissions.

Of course, I am not qualified to discuss the science of climate change, for I am not a scientist or a film star or a member of the British royal family or a former candidate for the presidency of the United States. Although I am aware that the science of climate change is far from fully understood and that several eminent scientists dissent from the so-called consensus view, I will assume that, on the whole, the scientific consensus is broadly correct and that man-made emissions of carbon dioxide will result in some rise in average global temperatures over the course of this century. Yet even if we grant this assumption, the conclusions of the radical Greens do not follow because there is no foundation for the second and third points concerning the likely impact of climate change and the way it is distributed between countries and generations.

The Damage Done by Climate Change

It seems quite likely that, *for the world as a whole,* the beneficial effects of moderate global warming in the range predicted by the IPCC will outweigh the harmful effects chiefly because global warming will increase food production in what are currently temperate or cold regions of the world. Some regions will be opened up for agricultural production, and growing seasons will be extended in vast areas, such as the northern states of the United States, Canada, Russia, and China. Also, higher carbon concentrations in the atmosphere will raise crop yields. Furthermore, for the world as a whole, global warming means more rain (or snow), and increasing cloud cover means that many parts of the world will be cooler during the day and warmer at night, leading to greater soil moisture, as has been observed in many states in the agricultural heartland of the United States (Balling 1992: 111).[30]

Given that climate change can have favorable as well as unfavorable effects, and in view of the enormous obstacles to sound predictions of climate change for individual regions, it is not surprising that most experts are agnostic as to the likely net damage *for the world as a whole* that might result from climate change. For example, in its recent report on climate change the Royal Commission on Environmental Pollution (RCEP) quotes William Nordhaus, one of the most respected economists to have studied the economic impact of climate change in great depth, as saying that "It must be emphasized that attempts to estimate the impacts of climate change continue to be highly speculative. Outside of agriculture and sea-level rise for a small number of countries, the number of scholarly studies of the economic impacts of climate change remains vanishingly small" (RCEP 2000: 51).

Nordhaus's estimates (Nordhaus 1994), which are in line with those suggested by the IPCC, suggest that world output will be reduced only by between approximately 1 to 2 percent by the year 2100 (assuming a doubling of carbon dioxide [CO_2] concentrations by then).[31] If the above predictions that world incomes per head around the year 2100 will be at least four times as high as they are now are anything like correct, this reduction in output is a trivial sacrifice. It corresponds to about one years' growth of output. In other words, in the year 2100 people will have to wait until 2101 in order to enjoy the standard of living that they would otherwise have enjoyed had there been no climate change. I am sure they will adjust to their disappointment.

It is true that the impact of a moderate rise in temperature on developed countries, which are mainly in temperate or cooler zones, is likely to be beneficial, whereas the impact on developing countries where average temperatures are higher, soils are often poorer, and technology and infrastructures are far less developed, is likely to be harmful. But this means that faster economic development in these countries helps them adapt to climate change. Estimates of the impact of climate change that assume that farmers are stupid and incapable of any adaptation to climate variations inevitably exaggerate the damage that might be done by climate change. And there are both theoretical reasons and empirical evidence for the view that the more developed an economy is, the greater the adaptation to climate change (Mendelsohn and Dinar, 1999; Mendelsohn, Dinar, and Sanghi, 2001).

Of course, wild assertions are made about the dire impact of climate change on developed countries, including predictions of more severe storms and climate instability or the spread of diseases that are now confined largely to tropical climates. As regards the former, it is often asserted that climate change will lead to an increase in the frequency and severity of storms and their accompanying damage to life and property. But it might lead to fewer storms. Theoretically, the latter happens to be more likely. The reports of the IPCC are neutral on the matter.

According to one of the IPCC working groups: "Some in the insurance industry perceive a current trend toward increased frequency and severity of extreme climate events. Examination of the meteorological data fails to support their perception in the context of a long-term change" (IPCC 1996a: 11).[32] As the eminent scientist Bert Bolin—who was, until recently, the chairman of the IPCC—points out, "Environmental activists, for example, seize eagerly on the occurrence of extreme events (hurricanes, floods, droughts, etc.) as signs of an ongoing change of climate. Even though extreme events may be harbingers of change, there is still as yet little scientific evidence to prove this, nor can we as yet ascribe such changes to human interference" (1997: 107).[33]

In fact, far from an increase in storms, there has been some evidence of a downward trend in the frequency of storms (Henderson-Sellers et al. 1997; Landsea et al. 1996; Schiesser et al. 1997). Of course, the damage done by a storm of any given intensity is likely to be greater today than it was fifty or even ten years earlier, but only because there are more buildings around to be damaged and their prices are much higher.[34]

There is equally little substance to the claim that climate change will lead to a return of insect-spread diseases, such as dengue fever and malaria, to temperate countries. In a recent article in *The Lancet*, Paul Reiter, the chief scientist of the Dengue Fever Branch of the Centers for Disease Control, writes that "The distortion of science to make predictions of unlikely public health disasters diverts attention from the true reasons for the recrudescence of vector-borne diseases. These include large-scale resettlement of people, rampant urbanization without adequate infrastructure . . . and the deterioration of vector-control operations and other public-health practices" (1998: 839). In developed countries, deaths from such diseases account for only 1 percent of all deaths, although these diseases were widespread in such countries in the past before they attained their present levels of affluence. For example, malaria and cholera were major health problems in the United States in the nineteenth century; and malaria was widespread in southern Europe until the mid–twentieth century, when good health practices and the use of insecticides and drainage programs wiped out large mosquito-breeding areas.

In fact, even ignoring the contribution of economic growth, up to a point a warmer climate is likely to reduce mortality and disease in developed countries. A recent authoritative study of German mortality statistics in the last half of the twentieth century showed that colder weather is a more significant killer than hotter weather (Lerchl 1998). Similar results were found in a British study, which came to the conclusion that, ceteris paribus, a rise in average annual temperature of 3 degrees Celsius would reduce annual mortality in Britain by 17,500 (Bentham 1997: 89). Of course, all such estimates are subject to a large margin of error. Nevertheless, they establish the point that, contrary to the impression given in much alarmist literature, a moderate rise in temperature is likely to decrease disease and mortality rather than increase them.

The Costs of Combating Climate Change

How the costs of reducing carbon emissions compare with the costs (if there are net costs) of anthropic climate change is rarely discussed in public debate, probably for two main reasons. First, the harmful effects of global warming appear to be too uncertain for any comparison to be made between them and the costs of reducing carbon emissions. Second, it is widely assumed that the case for maintaining the carbon concentration in the atmosphere as near as possible to current levels can be grounded in some notions of intergenerational justice that impose on us an obligation to bequeath to future generations the same environment we enjoy now. This argument implies that the economist's cost-benefit approach is irrelevant because it will be overruled by appeal to the inalienable "rights" of future generations. I believe that this argument is flawed, for reasons set out in chapter 7. Anyway, rightly or wrongly, the politics of global warming and the public's perception of the ethics are such that political leaders in most countries—at least in the developed countries—generally regard some cut in carbon emissions as desirable so that all that needs to be discussed is how much, how fast, and who should shoulder the burden.

But the fact remains that estimates of the size of the burden of reducing carbon emissions are also subject to a multiplicity of uncertainties because of the very wide range of different assumptions that can reasonably be made about the timing of the measures taken, their severity, the assumed prices of the relevant fuels, the costs of the carbon-free substitutes, the ease of substitution between energy and other inputs (capital and labor), the growth of world output and incomes, the extent to which restrictions on energy consumption feed back on output growth, and the type of measures used to reduce carbon emissions (notably taxes or tradable permits as compared with regulation). As can be imagined, a wide variety of models have been used to estimate likely economic costs and benefits under different assumptions.[35]

Comparisons between models are made particularly difficult, of course, because they often relate to different time periods or because they assume different reductions in carbon emissions. Nevertheless, given the wide range of assumptions that can reasonably be made, it is surprising that there is not even more variation in the results obtained than has been the case. For example, whereas two of the main models give estimates of the loss of GWP for the year 2100, one of the estimates relates to a 50 percent cut in carbon emissions and the other to a 75 percent cut (Mabey et al. 1997: 74). The former estimate arrives at a reduction in GWP of only 1 percent, and the latter puts the reduction at 5 percent. But given the latter's assumption of a much greater cut in carbon emissions, and given that the unit costs of reducing carbon emissions probably rise exponentially the greater the cuts, these estimates are not wildly out of line (Mabey et al. 1997: 78).

It is true that there is also scope for what is known as "no-regret" policies—that is, policies to reduce carbon emissions that have no costs and may even have benefits. This is the case, for example, where excessive carbon emissions result from the bad tax or subsidy policies that prop up obsolete industries or production techniques—especially in coal and steel production—that are heavy emitters of carbon. Elimination of such subsidies will bring benefits, not incur costs, and will also help reduce carbon emissions. But such policies cannot, by themselves, significantly attenuate the future increase in carbon concentrations in the atmosphere.

Nevertheless, all the various estimates of the costs of cutting carbon emissions point to their amounting to a very small percentage of world output—that is, of the order of 1 to 2 percent, which, as we have seen, is roughly the same order of magnitude of the likely damage that might be done by climate change.

Climate Change: The Overall Balance and Its Distribution

In view of these estimates, it is not surprising that Nordhaus's 1994 model and its subsequent refinements and extensions, which constitute the very few detailed studies of what would be an economically "optimal" policy to reduce carbon emissions, show that very few cuts in global carbon emissions are justified by a comparison of the costs and benefits. Taking together the costs and benefits of policies to restrain carbon emissions and adopting discount rates in the region of 4 percent, which seems to be the minimum one can reasonably adopt given the rate of return on other investments, these models show that only moderate restrictions on carbon emissions are justified (in addition to "no-regret" policies) *for the world as a whole.* Compared to an estimated present value of a loss of world income if carbon concentrations double their present levels of nearly $5 trillion, the cost of stabilizing carbon *emissions* at recent levels would be nearly $9 trillion and the cost of trying to restrain the rise in temperature to 1.5°C would be over $37 trillion! (Nordhaus and Boyer, 2000: 7: 25).

But effective international measures to combat climate change will impose proportionately very heavy burdens on poor countries that desperately need economic growth. This means that they have an urgent need for increased energy consumption, part of which will have to be provided by greatly increased consumption of their indigenous supplies of coal or other high-carbon fossil fuels. As Deepak Lal points out, a 1996 IPCC report estimated that reductions in carbon emissions in less-developed countries might impose very great reductions in their gross national products (GNPs), reaching 13 percent over the next two decades in the case of China according to one scenario (1997: 83–92). Lal is surely right in arguing that the attempt by various pressure groups in rich countries to impose unwanted carbon reduction policies on poor countries is a modern form of imperialism.

Furthermore, the above discussion of two alleged effects of climate change—namely, the incidence of storms or of insect-borne disease—also illustrates how unattractive any sacrifice of economic growth in the interests of long-run reductions in global warming will be for countries that are poor today. For example, where storms have hit rich countries, their wealth and infrastructures have enabled them to cope, whereas when they have hit poor countries with inadequate infrastructures, the effects can be disastrous.

Similarly, in the developing countries, the main cause of disease and mortality is not the climate but poverty, with its attendant lack of drainage, clean water, sanitation, and public health infrastructures. The best safeguard for these countries, therefore, is economic growth. In fact, a recent report by the UN World Health Organization (WHO) states that "As the new millennium approaches, the global population has never had a healthier outlook" and that the only significant growing threat to human health is HIV/AIDS, which has no relationship to climate (1998: 1, Executive Summary). The WHO report surveys the enormous increase in life expectancy and the reduction of diseases and suffering over the course of the twentieth century, almost all of which can be traced to rising incomes.

Similarly, the American Council on Science and Health insists, in a recent survey of the alleged relationship between climate change and health, that "The optimal approach to dealing with the prospect of climate change would *(a)* include improvement of health infrastructures (especially in developing countries) and *(b) exclude any measures that would impair economies and limit public health resources*" (1997: 6, italics added). The former includes intensive cost-effective control of insect vectors and improvement in clean drinking water and sanitation in developing countries. The latter implies that what developing countries need is a rapid growth of incomes and hence an increased use of energy, not measures to hamper their growth in a short-sighted attempt to restrain their use of energy by more than the steady technological advance in energy saving is producing anyway. The report adds that "Regardless of whether human-induced climate change will occur, we need policies for coping with infectious diseases and severe weather impacts of natural origin" (7).

As the IPCC points out, "If we take aggressive action to limit climate change they [future generations] may regret that we did not use the funds instead to push ahead development in Africa, to better protect the species against the next retrovirus, or to dispose of nuclear materials safely" (1996b: 33). The future generations in these countries might also resent that the resources were not used to improve the general standards of living, education, health, and housing of their ancestors, which would have directly affected the quality of their own lives.

Schelling (1995) has brilliantly exposed the inconsistency in policies that are designed to raise the incomes of people who are distant from us in time but that do nothing for more needy people alive today. Countries such as China and India will probably be five to ten times richer in one hundred years' time than they are now, even with conservative estimates of their future growth rates. Given the reluctance in most advanced countries to increase aid to poorer countries today, Schelling is right in saying that "It would be strange to forgo a percent or two of GNP for 50 years [for example, in incurring costs of reducing carbon emissions] for the benefit of Indians, Chinese, Indonesians, and others who will be living 50 to 100 years from now—and probably much better off than today's Indians, Chinese, and Indonesians—and not a tenth of that amount to increase the consumption of contemporary Indians, Chinese, and Indonesians" (1995: 397). Thus, the imposition of any burdens on people alive today—which will inevitably impinge on the poorest—

in order to add a few percentage points to the incomes of their far richer descendants toward the end of the next century is an anti-egalitarian form of inverted ancestor worship, the irony of which will not be lost on the Chinese.

If one is seriously concerned with equity—as those who parade their devotion to the cause of sustainable development claim to be—it makes no sense to impose heavy burdens on today's generation in order to raise the welfare of people alive one hundred years from now. And if one takes account of the different groups of people who will benefit most from reduced global warming and those who will bear the costs of measures to reduce global warming, such measures are even more difficult to justify. The pretensions of the global warming lobby to occupy the moral high ground are a travesty of the truth.

None of this means that climate change should not be taken seriously. The above discussion has been addressed to the question of how much damage might be done by the sort of climate change that might take place during the course of this century. But, in the first place, even such estimates are subject to a high degree of uncertainty. In particular, little is understood about the way some of the feedback mechanisms in climate-change atmospheric physics work. They might moderate the rate of warming or increase it. And the latest IPCC report has slightly raised its estimate of the range of possible temperature increases over the course of the twenty-first century to between 1.4 and 5.8 degrees Celsius. Most of the economic estimates of the damage that climate change might produce are based on earlier IPCC estimates of this range, which were somewhat lower than those now put forward. If the actual global temperature rise turns out to be near the top end of the latest range, the effects will be greater than the costs and benefits assumed in the above discussion (IPCC 2001: 8). Instead of being in a roughly zero-sum game in which, for the world as a whole, the benefits from moderate climate change may almost outweigh the damage, we might be in a situation in which there is serious damage for almost everybody.

Second, given the very long lags in the climate-change process and the persistence of carbon molecules in the atmosphere for up to two hundred years, unless action is taken during the course of the next few decades to reduce the rate of carbon emissions, a degree of damage that might be easily accommodated by a much richer world if the global mean temperature rises by, say, 2 to 3 degrees Celsius by the end of this century might become far more serious if the temperature were to increase significantly throughout the following century. But technological developments leading to reductions in the carbon intensity of economic activity in the twenty-second century probably make all such projections totally irrelevant.

But suppose that all the above arguments about the balance between the costs and benefits of climate change on the basis of a rise of only approximately 2 to 3 degrees over the course of this century are much too optimistic. Does the possibility of exaggerated optimism justify taking immediate action rather than waiting until further progress has been made in understanding climate change? Does it justify running the risk of imposing heavy costs on the present generation rather than devoting more time, effort, and resources to helping the developing countries to overcome the environmental problems facing them today, not to mention many environmental problems in the richer countries? This is where environmentalist groups appeal to the precautionary principle.

5

The Precautionary Principle

Emergence of the Precautionary Principle

The precautionary principle has long been established as one of the basic principles of sustainable development. A strong version of the principle was adopted by the UN Economic Conference for Europe, the final Ministerial Declaration of which was that "In order to achieve sustainable development, policies must be based on the precautionary principle. Environmental measures must anticipate, prevent and attack the causes of environmental degradation. Where there are threats of serious or irreversible damage, lack of full scientific certainty should not be used as a reason for postponing measures to prevent environmental degradation" (qtd. in Morris 2000: 5).[36] And the obligation to take account of the principle is even incorporated as Article 130(R) in the 1992 Treaty on European Union (known as the Maastricht Treaty).

A slightly weaker version of the principle is enshrined in the 1992 UNCED Rio Declaration, Article 15 of which states that "Where there are threats of serious or irreversible damage, lack of full scientific certainty shall not be used as a reason for postponing cost-effective measures to prevent environmental degradation." This version has been adopted as standard in various other international conventions or agreements, including the UN Framework Convention on Climate Change and its related Kyoto Protocol, as well as the UN Convention on Biological Diversity. However, as Julian Morris has shown, even this weaker version of the precautionary principle is open to several objections. In particular it is not clear (1) what is meant by a "threat"; (2) whether "damage" is defined in such a way that all change is potentially damaging; and (3) how serious is "serious."

The Harmful Implications of the Precautionary Principle

The notion that there can be full scientific certainty about the consequences of any change in the environment is, of course, absurd, and if it had ever been taken seriously, we would still be living in the Stone Age. Even changes that environmentalists favor, such as the replacement of fossil fuels with other sources of energy—wind power, hydropower, and so on—will have environmental effects, and it would be impossible to prove that they would never have undesirable consequences. It would even be impossible to prove that there can never be any harmful consequences from far greater exploitation of solar energy.

In other words, in following the precautionary principle there is a danger that terrible mistakes might be made. For example, in the late 1960s there was a widespread alarm that the world was entering a new ice age. If policies had been adopted then to prevent it, they would have included, presumably, measures to stimulate further the growing use of fossil fuels, with consequences that, it is now widely believed, would have been catastrophic. More generally, if we had taken seriously the "authoritative" predictions of the imminent exhaustion of fossil fuels that, as noted in chapter 3, have been made for more than a hundred years, not only would many developments that rely on cheap energy have been stifled in the interests of energy conservation but, at the same time, many technological developments that permitted a vastly expanded discovery, exploitation, and use of sources of energy would have been banned. The world would be a very much poorer place.[37] And this poverty would not be the result simply of greatly reduced availability of all sorts of industrial goods. The harmful effects of applying the precautionary principle in the past would have included, for example, severe restrictions on thousands of innovations such as vaccines and antibiotics that have saved millions of lives.

In fact, this principle is just a pompous way of saying that one should consider the case for making some investments now in order to minimize the danger of some unpleasant event taking place later. But nobody in their senses would make investments to avoid *every* remote possibility since that would leave precious little for the enjoyment of life.

The harm that would have been done by application in the past of sustainable development policies and the attendant precautionary principle is only part of the story. We have been and still are witnessing today many harmful effects of such policies. In addition to the general effects of the application of the precautionary principle, especially increasing bureaucratization of human activities and increased protectionist pressures (to be discussed in chapter 6), there have been many concrete and particular instances of damage done by application of the principle.

The Precautionary Principle and Biotechnology

One extremely important example of damage done is the current widespread opposition to the biotechnical development in the field of genetically modified (GM) crops and the proliferation of UN programs and agencies that have proposed and implemented a wide range of unnecessary and harmful regulations governing the research into and the development of GM crops. The development of GM crops offers enormous benefits to farmers all over the world, including, in particular, farmers in developing countries. Crops that are more resistant to viruses and pests and that are also able to tolerate drier, hotter, and more saline conditions greatly reduce the risks of crop failures in many developing countries. "More than one billion people in the world now live on less than a dollar a day and hundreds of millions are severely malnourished. . . . By increasing the efficiency of agriculture and food production in myriad ways, recombinant DNA-derived products can significantly increase the availability and nutritional value of foods and reduce their cost. However, the application of the precautionary principle will stall progress and exact a substantial human toll" (Miller and Conko 2000: 100).

Furthermore, opposition to research into the development of GM foods is hampered not merely by the sort of ecoterrorists who have vandalized research laboratories and field trials of GM crops in

Britain and the United States. It is even more effectively hampered by respectable bureaucrats under the umbrella of the "code of conduct" for field trials drawn up by the UN Industrial Development Organization (UNIDO) in 1992 and by the steps taken that led to the final Biodiversity Protocol (BSP) agreed in Montreal in 2000. The parties to the agreement "agreed on a scheme that violates the principle that the degree of scrutiny should be commensurate with risk. The agreement singles out recombinant DNA-manipulated products for extraordinary regulatory scrutiny in spite of a total lack of evidence that such products deserve special attention" (Miller and Conko 2000: 94). The BSP appeals to the precautionary principle as set out in the 1992 UNCED Declaration and hence shifts the burden of proof from regulators, who had previously been required to prove that the crop was likely to be harmful, to the researchers and innovators, who must now prove that there is no possibility of any harm. But it is virtually impossible in theory to prove this sort of negative effect, and in practice (i.e., to satisfy the subjective risk/reward ratio of regulators) it is very costly.

As a result of the unthinking application of the precautionary principle, the costs of development in biotechnology will be higher, the associated risks will be greater, and the pace of progress will be slower. How many scientists and how many of the firms and institutes that back them will be prepared to accept the risks of researching GM technology when they may be prevented from applying the results of that research for reasons that have little to do with public health and more to do with pressures from protectionist and anti-technology groups backed up by a fearful public brainwashed by media hysteria? As Miller and Conko put it, the greatest effect of the Biodiversity Protocol "will be to hobble the work of academic researchers and small, innovative companies, ultimately delaying or denying the benefits of the 'gene revolution' to much of the world" (2000: 94).

The 1992 UNIDO code of conduct required the establishment of new environmental bureaucracies for purposes of regulating researchers. The skilled resources needed for this task are very scarce in developing countries. Not surprisingly, the UNIDO bureaucrats have been keen to offer their own services to countries that presently lack enough suitably qualified officials. More serious than this bit of rent seeking is the fact that developing countries are expected to use their own scarce resources to enforce the regulation of GM crop research instead of using them to combat known threats to human health, such as schistosomiasis, malaria, and other diseases associated with lack of clean water and sanitation, as well as AIDS, polio, cholera, and hepatitis (Miller and Conko 2000: 88).

In short, the GM crop story is a flagrant case of misused resources: resources that could have been put to good use are being diverted instead to warding off the perceived threat of some unforeseeable catastrophe that might conceivably result from technological innovation. Consumers in rich countries may not suffer all that much if they are denied the benefits that GM crops bring to them in the way of cheaper foods, but in poorer countries the consequences will be unnecessary hunger, disease, and death. It is another example, like the climate-change example discussed above, of a quasi-imperialist attitude to the problems of the Third World. It is typical of the intellectual confusion in the environmentalist movement that many of its more extreme activists attack the wicked capitalists and imperialists and related globalization while simultaneously pressuring governments to implement policies that can only impoverish developing countries—simply in order to pander to the prejudices of well-meaning but ill-informed people in the rich countries or to the "power-seeking" agendas of bureaucrats.

The alternative to the precautionary principle is not non-action but informed action. Drastic action to reduce climate change today, for example, is probably undesirable *given today's state of knowledge.* If we wait, however, new knowledge will arrive, and it will become much clearer what actions are best. The "look before you leap" argument is reinforced by the following considerations.

1. Delaying action by several years makes a negligible difference. A ten-year delay in switching over from the IPCC's "business as usual" scenario (i.e., no action taken to reduce global warming) to a tough anti-global warming scenario, for example, would increase the temperature by the year 2100 by only between 0.2 and 0.6 degrees Celsius, depending on whether one adopts the bottom or the top of the IPCC's latest estimate of the range of global warming

predictions. So if we delay action by ten years, the extra warming will probably be approximately 0.4°C by the year 2100, which gives us plenty of time to change into a lighter shirt.

2. There has been an explosion of research into climate change during the last few years so that we can expect major improvements in our knowledge of this phenomenon during the course of the next decade. It is thus much more sensible to support this research rather than rush to conclusions that might prove to be very expensive, particularly so in the light of the following economic considerations.

3. Reductions in the supply of some material relative to the demand do not have significant effects on the world economy as long as there is time for the economy to adapt. The market mechanism will produce incentives to find substitutes and to economize in its use. But if the change were to be dramatic—for example, if the world were to be obliged to cut its use of fossil fuels drastically—the effect will be extremely costly and possibly catastrophic. If, in the light of further scientific progress, it is found necessary to carry out any significant cut in energy use, it is far less costly to bring it about gradually, thereby giving the world time to invest in substitutes and in technological progress to economize in energy, and gradually to switch patterns of production and consumption into less energy-intensive forms. Large-scale draconian action is a recipe for economic disaster and tilts the balance of costs and benefits heavily on the wrong side.

4. Furthermore, as I have already shown, even without any special measures to curb energy consumption—indeed, even with a decline in the real price of most energy sources over the last decade or so—there has already been considerable technological progress in the exploitation of renewable energy resources and in methods of economizing in energy in general. A continued reduction in the costs of energy-economizing investment or in the use of nonpolluting renewable energy will mean that the costs of measures to cut energy use will be further reduced. It would be absurd, therefore, to press for rapid early cuts in energy consumption before taking advantage of cheaper methods of reducing this consumption that can be anticipated over the course of the next decade or so.

5. Because there is little point in any individual country trying to reduce global warming by itself, effective action to reduce global

warming depends on international agreement. It will be immensely difficult to reach any effective international agreement to reduce carbon emissions drastically if only because of the vast differences between countries with respect to how far they will lose or gain. This does not mean, however, that it is impossible to reach an agreement, but it does mean that a hastily contrived agreement is unlikely to be the most efficient one. Such an agreement will more likely impose quantitative limits on the carbon emissions of different countries than embody least-cost market mechanisms. Given more time, there is at least some chance that governments can agree on some sort of market-based mechanism for allocating carbon emission reductions among countries that will *(a)* minimize the total burden on the world economy and *(b)* ensure an equitable compensation for those countries—especially the developing countries—that will be least able to bear the costs.

A complex computer model is not needed to arrive at the conclusion that it is not worthwhile making expensive investments in measures to enforce rapid reductions in CO_2 emissions when the penalty for waiting is so small. What the precautionary principle slogan seems to imply, therefore, at least in this context, is "Take action now when it is very expensive and will hit very poor people in order to benefit less poor people in the distant future rather than wait a few years when technical progress will have made it much cheaper and we will have a much better idea of whether expensive action is necessary."

It goes almost without saying, however, that we should not delay in taking no-regret policies. In particular, in many countries large subsidies are paid to the production and use of coal, which is among the dirtiest forms of fossil fuel from the point of view of its carbon emissions. More generally, it is estimated that world subsidies for fossil fuels amount to approximately $230 billion, and in developing and "transition" economies alone, energy subsidies amount to nearly $200 billion.[38] Subsidies mean that resources are used in activities that have less value to society than do the resources in question. Eliminating such subsidies, therefore, adds to overall incomes. Measures might also be taken to reduce market failures that prevent research and innovation designed to promote energy savings and the development of renewable energy from attaining their socially optimal level. There is also scope for various methods of preventing carbon from reaching the atmosphere, including further progress in carbon sequestration and a move toward zero-emission power plants (Ausubel 1999; RCEP 2000: chap. 3).

Of course, the uncertainties concerning climate change work in both directions. For example, it is quite possible—and many energy experts think it probable—that the world will be emitting very little carbon anyway by the middle of the twenty-first century. As discussed in chapter 3, rapid advances are being made in technologies for obtaining energy from nonpolluting sources, such as wind power, solar energy, and hydrogen, especially when accompanied by more economic fuel cells. So it might well be that energy technology will be totally transformed during the course of this century and all the fears about rising temperatures into the year 2200 and beyond will turn out to have been totally unfounded. Major sacrifices now to cut consumption of fossil fuels will then turn out not merely to have been unjustified but to have led to a loss of economic growth and hence a prolongation of many of the consequences of world poverty.

All these uncertainties mean that, although I do not wish to condone the undue deference widely given to the precautionary principle, there is everything to be said for an old-fashioned economic approach to the problem. This approach involves an acceptance of risk aversion together with its implication that one should adopt a portfolio of policies, along the lines proposed by Bolin (1998). A prudent approach would be to adopt a portfolio of policies, including mitigation, adaptation, and research aimed at improving our knowledge of the processes involved, corresponding to the way that any well-run corporation or private household organizes its activities. But, of course, to most environmental pressure groups, normal business practices are anathema, and any excuse must be found for abandoning the market mechanism in favor of central planning and "command-and-control" policies.

6

Bureaucratic Regulation
and Protectionism

As mentioned above, at the 1992 UNCED, the countries adopted a document of several hundred pages, known as *Agenda 21*, which set out, among other things, the agreed intentions of the countries to take account of environmental objectives in their domestic policies; to monitor their own developments from the point of view of their sustainability, taking full account of environmental changes; and to submit regular reports on these developments to the newly established Commission on Sustainable Development (CSD), comprising fifty-three members and set up to monitor progress toward sustainable development.[39]

In addition to this UN commission, countless other institutes, government departments and NGOs, all professing to promote sustainable development, have been established all over the world. The World Bank, for example, now has a vice-president for environmentally sustainable development.

The UN has also set up three committees—namely, the Committee on Natural Resources, the Committee on New and Renewable Sources of Energy, and the Committee on Science and Technology for Development. Each of these committees spawned further committees. For example, the Committee on Natural Resources has recommended that a commission on mining and materials be established to assess and report on "technological progress toward sustainable resource use." It justifies the need for this additional commission on the grounds that "Continued growth in per capita consumption to levels currently enjoyed by the developed countries for a future global population of 10–12 billion is clearly not sustainable."[40] As shown in chapters 2 through 4, this statement flies in the face of all the evidence.

Bureaucratic Regulation Versus the Market in Environmental Policy

One of the worst consequences of excessive bureaucratic intervention in daily life is the bureaucratic preference for regulation rather than market mechanisms to deal with any social and economic problems. This is clearly the case in environmental protection. It is true that, until relatively recently, economic policy tended to neglect environmental issues, in particular those having very long-run consequences. It is right, therefore, that the environment (interpreted very loosely) should now be given its proper place in the conduct of policy. It makes a major contribution to human welfare in all sorts of ways—as a source of materials, of food, of spiritual and aesthetic satisfaction, of leisure activities, and so on.

But most of the oldest forms of excessive pollution in what are now the advanced countries of the world are usually the result of an inadequate specification of property rights. For example, if a firm freely pollutes a stream with its effluent or the air with gases and smoke from its chimneys, it is reducing the amount of clean water or clean air available to other people without this being the outcome of any negotiated bargain between the firm and the victims of the pollution. The polluter is in effect using up, free of charge, a scarce resource, namely clean air or clean water, in a way that imposes costs on other members of society in various forms. These costs may include tangible damages, such as to health, fish catch, corrosion of metals, and so on, or simple intangible loss of welfare on account of the destruction of an otherwise pleasant environment.

The optimal way of dealing with such pollution is to make the polluter pay the cost to society of such damage. In that way, the polluter will use up the environment only to the point where the marginal damage done is covered by the marginal benefit to the firm (and to society) of using the resource in question. There are various ways in which such an outcome can be achieved. One is to impose pollution charges—that is, a tax levied per unit of pollution. Another is to arrange a negotiation between the polluters and the victims that should lead to a price being fixed that, at the margin, will compensate the victims for the damage they suffer. There are equity questions to be settled, of course, such as who really has the property rights in the environmental medium in question. But that is a separate matter that lies outside our scope here. The point is that an economic instrument of one kind or another can help move toward a socially optimal level of pollution.

A more relevant point here is some philosophers' assertion that the use of the price mechanism to restrict pollution fails to recognize the fundamentally immoral character of pollution—an assertion widely accepted in environmental circles (Goodin 1994; Sandel 1997). It is argued that allowing people to pollute as long as they pay for the right to do so is akin to the medieval practice of allowing people to buy indulgences. The price mechanism would detract from the moral opprobrium that, in these philosophers' view, ought to be attached to the polluting activity.

But, as explained above, the harm done by pollution is the inefficient use of a scarce resource, which may be clean air, clean water, unspoilt scenery, and so on.[41] If the resource in question is not scarce, no harm is done. There is no sin without victims, or, at least, potential victims. The human race has had to use water since the beginning of its existence, but only when and where it is scarce is any harm done on account of somebody else suffering from being deprived of supplies of the resource in question. Thus, it is in a completely different category from conventional sins for which indulgences may have been bought, for in the latter cases the sin exists without any limitation on the supply of sinfulness. For example, adultery has long been regarded as a sin, but one person's adultery (or should I say two people's adultery?) does not reduce the total amount of adultery that other people can commit.

But the moral arguments against the use of market mechanisms to restrict pollution have had far less influence than a variety of economic arguments that have also been used throughout the years—and are still used by bureaucrats and by less-enlightened environmental activists—to deny the value of market mechanisms and to support the use of regulations. It would be out of place to review all these economic arguments here.[42]

It is true that the efficacy of market-based mechanisms relies on somebody having an economic incentive not to use the resource more than is socially optimal. Despite the high value of cattle, sheep, and goats, there is no threat to their existence because someone owns these animals and as a result takes steps to protect them. The fact that these animals are used commercially, however, is not the relevant factor. The buffalo herds owned by the environmentalist Ted Turner are similarly protected, as are animals on property owned by the Nature Conservancy and other environmental groups. What is needed is a regime of clearly established property rights. It is true that it is often technically difficult to establish property rights for certain resources, so that market-based solutions for environmental problems are not always easy to apply.

Where some resource is regarded as a common property, no individual has an incentive to limit his or her use of it. Indeed, if the common property in question is also limited in supply, everybody has an incentive to use it up as quickly as possible before other people use it all up. The principle of "first come, first serve" rules the day. For example, the poaching of rhinos in the poachers' rush to get them first has resulted in a drastic fall in their numbers in Africa. And threats to fishery stocks are widespread in many parts of the world, particularly in waters fished by many members of the European community.

Such cases provide a wonderful pretext for advocates of sustainable development to claim that only special regulations and governmental control can prevent the extinction of many endangered species, such as elephants, rhinos, and fish stocks. However, in most cases it is by no means technically impossible to confer property rights or some economic stake in the conservation of the resources in question. For example, in South Africa, Botswana, and Zimbabwe, where the local people have been given a stake in the economic value of elephants—for tourism or for sale of the tusks—the incentive to protect and conserve or to increase elephant stocks appears to have been very effective (Ridley 1995: 51–52; Sugg and Kreuter 1994: *passim*).

And there are many other instances—in addition to obvious cases such as cattle—of the conservation of species of animals as a result of the operation of property rights, including minks (North 2000: *passim*); ostriches, crocodiles, and vicuna, which had hitherto been an endangered species ('t Sas-Rolfes 1995: 53–54); and oysters and other aquaculture (d'Auria et al. 1999: 18).

Even fishing, which might appear to be a clear case where it is virtually impossible to apply market-based solutions, has proved to be amenable to such solutions in countries where they have been tried, notably in Australia and New Zealand, and are being taken up by other countries (Ridley 1996). The chief feature of such solutions has been the allocation to fishermen of a share—based on their previous catch—in the total quantity of fish that is allowed to be landed each year. But the fishermen are entitled to sell their shares if they wish, so that they now own an asset, the value of which is greater the higher are fish stocks in the seas and hence the total amount that is allowed to be landed. They now have an incentive to preserve the market value of their shares by maintaining the stocks of fish in the seas. They then become part owners of a resource rather than competitors in a scramble to scoop up the fish before somebody else does. They have an incentive to help monitor destruction of the fish stocks by others. As Matt Ridley puts it, there is nothing to stop the European community from introducing such a system "except its philosophy, which is that individuals are not to be trusted with property, only institutions and states" (1996: 12).

The normal bureaucratic response to such problems is, of course, to introduce regulations, and in spite of paying lip service to the market, very few governments have resorted to market-based instruments to deal with environmental problems.[43] And combined with misguided pressures from environmental groups, regulations rather than market-based solutions have also extended to international trade: for example, the bans on the trade in ivory and other products enshrined in the UN Convention on International Trade in Endangered Species (CITES) or the European community's Common Fisheries policy, with its government-enforced regulation of net sizes, boat numbers, and so on. Yet the history of such regulatory policies is one of failure, for they do not give anybody an economic incentive to conserve and protect the resource in question. On the contrary, banning the trade in elephants' ivory has merely encouraged poachers to make profits out of illegal trade, as has been the case in many African countries. Reliance on negative incentives such as prohibition of hunting or sale of ivory is usually ineffective even in rich countries with plenty of resources for law enforcement, as the experience of prohibition in the United States demonstrated. In poor countries, the resources available for the enforcement of regulations are far scarcer, and corruption is not exactly unknown.

Economics and the Value of the Environment

None of the above means that there is no need for governments to take action to improve environmental conditions in many parts of the world. Poor environmental conditions—notably as regards clean drinking water, sanitation, and decent shelter—are a major cause of misery, disease, squalor, and degradation for hundreds of millions of people throughout the world (Beckerman 1992a, 1992b). Where severe poverty is the crux of the problem, market-based solutions cannot be relied on to provide poor people with the standards of certain facilities that humanitarian concern for human welfare would regard as minimal. Even in rich countries, many environmental problems arise on account of the "public good" character of the facilities in question. Thus, to the urgent need to improve local environmental conditions in the Third World can be added the needs for expenditures to improve the urban environment almost everywhere, as well as some components of the global environment, notably the oceans and the atmosphere.

Hence, from any perspective there are legitimate needs for expenditures on the protection and improvement of the environment, but this implies large-scale competition with expenditures on other sources of human welfare, such as health, education, shelter, and so on, because resources are limited. It is characteristic of the inconsistency in the arguments put forward for sustainable development that although we are warned, against all the evidence, of the danger that the world will run out of resources in the long run, no account is taken of the fact that, in the short run, resources *are* limited; which happens to be indisputable. Hence, society must find rational ways of allocating resources between, on the one hand, environmental conservation or improvement and, on the other hand, many other major objectives.

It is true that some features of the environment may be a source of top-level, intrinsic values, such as aesthetic or spiritual satisfaction. But so may many other goods or services—such as works of art, musical performances, books, and so on. Many ordinary goods and services—such as hospitals, schools, the institutions of law and order, dwellings, churches, libraries, and public buildings of all kinds—and plain basic private consumer goods may contribute to other equally important and often far more important top-level intrinsic values, such as our keeping alive and healthy, enjoying general personal well-being, and living in a society characterized by justice, liberty, the pursuit of knowledge, and human progress. In other words, the environment has to share with most other ordinary goods and services the capacity to provide us with instrumentally useful inputs into our most important values.

Thus, there is no case for attributing special status to certain aesthetic environmental assets that give them "trumping" power over innumerable other claims on resources. Nor is there any ethical justification for public bodies to have a bias in favor of the private preferences of some citizens for certain environmental assets, such as beautiful scenery, as against the private preferences of other citizens for other assets, such as decent housing, schools, health and education services, and so on. Of course, it may well be that the scale of preferences for the former will, in particular cases, justify greater provision for them. And in a decent society that aims at some degree of social cohesion, minority tastes must not be excluded, but this point ought not to be confused with an ethical case for their being given special priority.

Sustainable Development and Protectionism

Thus, pursuit of the goal of sustainable development is not merely harmful because it is responsible for proliferating a vast network of bureaucracies and waste of resources in research into or administration of sustainable-development policies. Many of the bureaucrats and economists in search of a mission might be doing far worse things than wasting their time with sustainable development. The trouble is that their resistance to market-based solutions to environmental problems and their predilection for regulation slows down the effective protection of the environment and aggravates resource misallocation.

The pursuit of sustainable development is particularly damaging for poorer countries because of the support that it provides for protectionist policies. Under the banner of sustainable development and environmental conservation, many groups in rich countries urge their governments to restrict imports of certain products from other countries—in particular poor countries—on the ground that the latter are failing in their duty to protect and preserve their environments. It is argued that lax environmental standards in some countries give them an "unfair" competitive advantage over countries that impose tougher environmental standards on their own producers. The former are accused of "unfairly" subsidizing their exports. Hence, there is much support for appeals such as that made by Senator Boren of Oklahoma, the proponent of the International Pollution Deterrence Act of 1991, who demanded import duties on the grounds that he saw "the unfair advantage enjoyed by other nationals exploiting the environment and public health for economic gain when I look at many industries important to my own state" (Bhagwati 1993: 20). Similarly, former Vice-President Al Gore has written that "weak and ineffectual enforcement of pollution control measures should also be included in the definition of unfair trading practices" (Bhagwati 1993: 20).

In other words, under the banner of sustainable development, governments are urged to adopt protectionist policies that resemble the long-standing protectionist pressures to restrict imports from low-wage countries. Consequently, insofar as environmentalists' activities either imply or directly call for a weakening of the international system of free trade built up over the years through the General Agreement on Trade and Tariffs (GATT, which was the precursor of what is now the World Trade Organization [WTO]), they often find allies in protectionist business and trade union interests. For a century or more, such policies have been sure of a warm welcome by many sections of society who will benefit from them in the short run. By contrast, the vast mass of the population in rich countries who will lose by them, namely all consumers, cannot easily organize themselves in opposition to specific items of protectionism or even—in many cases—realize that they will be the victims.

But perhaps the most immoral effect of the protectionist pressures exerted in the name of sustainable development is that the damage done to consumers in rich countries is proportionately much smaller than the damage done to the poor in developing countries. Measures that penalize exports from poor countries that do not adopt the environmental standards of rich countries harm these countries, whether they lose exports earnings or buckle under and adopt environmental policies that are not best for them given their state of development. Rich people are willing to give up some wealth for better environmental quality and even to know that some animal they may never see in the wild nevertheless exists. Most people in poor countries rate having a roof over their heads, a square meal in the next twenty-four hours, and clean water to drink as more important than the level of carbon in the atmosphere in fifty years' time. Most of them will not live that long. There is no virtue in seeking to punish other countries that do not give the same priority to environmental protection as may be desirable in rich countries.

Developing countries have a far more desperate need to expand exports and to develop their economies. Yet, in the name of sustainable development, the environmental movement has been very active in urging tough action against countries that do not follow the environmental policies that members of the movement would like. A striking example resulted from the decision in 1992 of the GATT Dispute Settlement Panel that ruled in favor of Mexico over the tuna fishing dispute (the United States had placed an embargo on the import of Mexican tuna on the grounds that the fish had been caught in purse seine, which killed dolphins in greater numbers than U.S. laws permit for U.S. fishing fleets).[44] Following the GATT ruling, a coalition of environmental groups placed an advertisement in the *New York Times* (20 April 1992) that was a vicious attack on GATT, which it accused—among other things—of mounting "a sneak attack on democracy."

In recent years, moreover, under the banner of sustainable development certain international treaties have been negotiated that are arguably in contravention of GATT, notably the Convention on International Trade in Endangered Species. Furthermore, aided in some cases by protectionist interests, including trade unions and some international bureaucratic institutions, notably within the European Union, the environmental movement has, in fact, succeeded in mounting a concerted international attack on the principles that have been operated with a fair degree of success by GATT since its inception. This attack has included pressure from various European countries (notably members of the Nordic Council and the European Union) to expand the exemptions in GATT Articles XX and XXIV to incorporate environmental concerns.

Expansion of these exceptions to include failure by any country to satisfy the environmental concerns of others will be a major retreat from the liberalization of international trade and will lead to a serious cut in living standards of rich and especially poor countries.

Of course, some will argue that the environment other countries are damaging is part of our common heritage and not just the property of the countries in question. In other words, it was alright for the inhabitants of temperate developed countries to cut down their forests over the last few centuries in order to make way for arable agriculture to feed their expanding populations, but now that some developing countries want to do the same, it is found that forests are a common heritage and that coercive action, such as banning imports of their timber, must be taken to stop it.

It may well be true that richer countries—or at least some sections of their populations—see themselves as deriving more satisfaction from knowing that tropical forests are being preserved than from using the timber. In that case, they are perfectly entitled to try to discourage other countries from cutting down their forests, if necessary by providing them with some form of economic incentive to refrain from doing so. But there is no case for using official aid for this purpose rather than for establishing some constructive purpose that directly helps the poorer people in the countries in question. As Deepak Lal puts it, "It is double immoral . . . to transfer aid funds to save plants rather than people, and to reduce further the future income growth prospects of the poor by promoting the growth-reducing programme of 'sustainable development'" (1990: 39).

Also, there is no reason why the taxpayers in rich countries should contribute to an action that is in the interests only of minority groups who happen to attach a particularly high "existence value" to certain environmental assets. Many taxpayers in rich countries will have higher priorities. After all, nothing prevents people who have a strong private preference for preserving rain forests or their indigenous species from organizing voluntary contributions to help such preservation in the same way that many charitable organizations exist so that people can make donations to help starving or sick children overseas. But coercion to impose the environmental values of some groups of people in the developed world on the people of other countries is indefensible.

It is true that there are no precise formulae for drawing boundary lines between different moral values in order to say which justify international action in their defense and which do not. For example, there may be a clear case for outlawing imports produced by slave labor, but a less clear case for outlawing imports produced with the aid of child labor because such restrictions can have harmful effects on the children and their families. But it is most unlikely that a case can be made out on any ethical grounds for a unilateral or multilateral suspension of other countries' trading rights in the defense of what must be second-order ethical preferences—such as a preference for dolphins over the livelihood of Mexican fishermen or for trees over food for poor communities in Thailand or Brazil. In any case, the slippery slope in the area of environmental preferences is too obvious, so that there can be an endless succession of demands for punitive trade restrictions on environmentalist grounds. "Environmentalists favor dolphins; Indians have their sacred cows. Animal rights activists, who do not prefer one species over another, will object to our slaughterhouses" (Bhagwati 1993: 19).

If other countries are to be "punished" in some way for failure to respect universal basic values, we should take into consideration that many of them indulge in far worse crimes against humanity than cutting down their trees. Yet these violations of basic and universally accepted human rights do not seem to arouse the same indignation among the environmental protectionists that they feel regarding the failure of overseas governments to attach an overriding importance to the environment. In the same way that for some people excessive love of animals is the counterpart of hatred of human beings, in some people an excessive concern with future generations is the counterpart of indifference to the suffering of people alive today.

7

The "Ethics" of
Sustainable Development

Sustainable Development and Our Obligations to Future Generations

> Individual interests are the only real interests. . . . Can it be conceived that there are men so absurd as to . . . prefer the man who is not, to him who is; to torment the living under presence of promoting the happiness of those who are not born, and who may never be born.
>
> —Jeremy Bentham (1843)[45]

Two main claims are usually made on behalf of the goal of sustainable development. First, it is alleged that continued economic growth will lead to the exhaustion of finite resources or some environmental catastrophe so that, in the longer run, the human race will be doomed to dire poverty. In chapters 2 through 4, I gave reasons to believe that this assertion is unfounded. The second claim—which is in part related to the first—is that only sustainable development respects the rights of future generations to inherit a satisfactory environment and hence better reflects the demands of intergenerational justice or equity. For this reason, sustainable development, it is argued, occupies the moral high ground. As one authority on the concept of sustainability bluntly puts it, "Sustainability is primarily an issue of intergenerational equity" (Norgaard 1992: 1).

But, in fact, this claim is at best an illusion, and at worst it is humbug. I have given some examples of how some of the policies advocated in the name of sustainable development would have prevented economic growth in the past and hence led to far lower standards of living than are enjoyed today. I have also given examples of the way that sustainable development is used as an excuse for policies that would have—and still do—hurt those sections of the world community that are most vulnerable.

For example, environmental preservation is often used as an excuse for protectionist pressures that will further impoverish poorer developing countries. Similarly, policies to enforce drastic reductions in carbon emissions in order to reduce climate change and to respect the exigencies of the precautionary principle will also hit developing countries particularly heavily. All these policies that are advocated in the name of sustainable development represent, in the end, a new form of imperialism: an attempt to control markets for the benefit of the products of Western industry and an attempt to impose the preferences of affluent groups in rich countries on other countries whether they like it or not. Sustainable development, therefore, has practical implications that would be morally unacceptable even if its ethical foundations were valid in theory. But, as is argued in this chapter, they are not even that.

Consider first the argument that only sustainable development respects the rights of future generations to inherit an environment that is no worse that the one we live in today—or, in other words, that it makes equitable allowance for the way that welfare is distributed between different generations. This alleged concern with equity is, in fact, often contrasted with the standard economist's concern with simply maximizing the future stream of utility over some relevant time period. For example, one of the leading authorities on Green political philosophy writes that the objective of sustainable development "contrasts with the directive of ordinary expected-utility maximization to go for the highest total payoff without regard to its distribution interpersonally or intertemporally" (Goodin 1983: 1).

The objective of maximizing society's total welfare (for a given population) is open to two objections. First, it could imply violating some basic rights—e.g., the individual's right to dispose of his property as he wishes, or work or live where he likes, or even more fundamental rights to life and liberty. Secondly, it could imply "excessive" inequality in the distribution of welfare. These two objections are, of course, familiar from the standard critiques of Utilitarianism.

And in the intertemporal context the objective of maximizing welfare over time (given the population) might imply that future generations inherit fewer environmental assets than exist today or that per capita welfare might rise for a time with economic growth but might eventually have to decline. According to sustainable development theorists, however, both these consequences are unacceptable. For they would violate the assumed rights of future generations to inherit the same environment as we have today and the requirements of intergenerational equality. But I argue in this chapter that (i) future generations have no rights and (ii) intergenerational egalitarianism is an indefensible objective. In that case there is no longer any reason to replace the economists' standard objective of maximizing welfare by the sustainable development objective. I argue, in other words, that the standard objections to maximizing total welfare do not apply in the intertemporal context (for fuller discussion, see Beckerman and Pasek, 2001, chapters 2–4).

The argument that future generations do not have rights and that intergenerational egalitarianism is indefensible does not mean that the interests of future generations ought not to be given any weight in current policy. The point is that their interests have no "trumping" power such as is conferred by "rights" or distributional constraints. The interests that they will have must take their place in the balance together with the interests of people alive today, many of whom live in dire poverty.

Sustainable Development Versus Maximizing Future Welfare

As explained in chapter 1, the most widely accepted concept of sustainable development is that the path of development should not include any periods in which there is a decline in per capita welfare. So we have to begin by asking, What is the moral force of a general rule that excludes future declines in welfare at any period of time even if it may be necessary to pay this price for higher levels of welfare before or after that point in time and even if the decline is from a much higher level of welfare than that prevailing today?

Such a rule would certainly not have much appeal as far as individual decisions about one's life plans are concerned. Many people, students for example, are prepared to accept a temporary decline in their welfare because they believe it is the path to a much higher total cumulative welfare over the whole of their lives. Some people may also opt for a very high standard of living in the shorter run even if they know full well that it cannot last indefinitely.

Of course, if we are *starting from any particular level* of anything desirable, such as per capita "welfare," it is better for it to go up or even to remain stable than to go down, but that is only because and insofar as we expect that this trend will lead to greater welfare per capita over the future than it would otherwise be. Yet it is perfectly feasible, even starting from the same level, for a path that did not contain any periods of declining per capita welfare to lead to lower per capita welfare over the whole period than a path that does contain a period of declining per capita welfare.

Consider, for example, figure 1, in which there are taken to be two alternative feasible paths of development. One of them, path SD, contains no periods of declining per capita welfare and so is a sustainable-development path. The other path, MSW, is the path that maximizes (feasible) per capita welfare over the whole period. On this path, earlier generations use up more resources and achieve higher standards of living than on the SD path, and as a result some future generations have less welfare than earlier generations. Yet almost every generation has a higher level of per capita welfare under the MSW path than under the SD path. But proponents of SD would be obliged to prefer the SD path even though a large majority of all the individuals alive during this time frame would prefer the MSW path. It seems unlikely that any ethical principle might be found to justify the SD choice.[46] The sustainable-development requirement to exclude any future declines in per capita welfare, at any price in terms of total cumulative welfare, thus seems to be utterly senseless.

In order to justify preferring sustainability to the maximization of per capita welfare over the future, therefore, appeal would have to be made to some ethical values other than welfare. What could

FIGURE 1
Why Must the SD Path Be Preferred to the MSW Path?

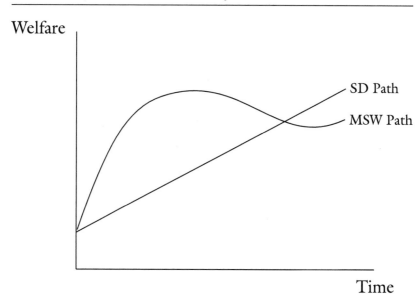

Welfare

SD Path

MSW Path

Time

these values be? If future generations can be shown to have *rights* to a level of per capita welfare that is no lower than that achieved by any previous generation, then such rights would trump simple welfare maximization. Or maximization might possibly be trumped by a claim of intergenerational justice or equity.

Do Future Generations Have Rights?

It seems doubtful that a future generation can have a right to a level of welfare at least as high as the previous generation.[47] Certainly no individual can be said to have such a right. Does every son have a right to at least as high a level of welfare as the father? And if this is nonsense on an individual level, it is difficult to see how aggregating the wealth of all parents and all children suddenly makes the right sensible.

More generally it is difficult to see how future generations can be said to have *any* rights because properties, such as being green or wealthy or having rights, can be predicated only of some subject that exists.[48] Propositions such as "X is Y" or "X has Z" or "X prefers A to B" make sense only if there is an X. If there is no X, then all such propositions are meaningless.[49] If I were to say "X has a fantastic collection of CDs," and you were to ask me who is X, and I were to reply, "Well, actually there isn't any X," you would think I had taken leave of my senses. And you would be right. Thus, the general proposition that future generations cannot have anything, including rights, follows from the meaning of the present tense of the verb *to have*.[50] Unborn people simply cannot *have* anything. They cannot have two legs or long hair or a taste for Mozart.

In connection with the more specific justification given for the goal of sustainable development—namely, that future generations have rights to specific assets, such as the existing environment and all its creatures—a second condition has to be satisfied. This condition is that even people who do exist cannot have rights to anything unless, in principle, the rights can be fulfilled (Parfit 1984: 365). For example, the dodo became extinct approximately three hundred years ago, so it would be absurd to claim that we have a right to see a live dodo.

Thus, for the proposition "X has a right to Y" to be valid, where Y refers to some tangible object, two essential conditions have to be satisfied. First, X must exist, and second, it must be possible, in principle, to provide Y.

In the case of our right to see live dodos, for example, one of these two conditions is not satisfied. We exist, but dodos do not exist. And before the dodos became extinct, the other condition was not satisfied: the dodos existed, but we did not, so we could not have any rights to its preservation. Hence, insofar as it is implausible to say that we *had* the right to the preservation of live dodos before we existed, it must be implausible to say that nonexistent unborn generations have any rights now. And it would also be implausible to say that, when these generations do exist, they will have any rights to some assets that do not then exist. Hence, it is doubly absurd to say that future generations have rights now to inherit any particular asset that may not exist in the future. In short, however widely society wishes to draw the boundary around the rights that future generations *will* have, these generations cannot *have* any rights now. Nor, when they come into existence, can the rights that they will have include rights to something that may no longer exist, such as an extinct species.

Now it may seem that this view of rights can have shocking implications for certain long-range environmental problems. Suppose, for example, that somebody had made preparations to set off a bomb in, say, two hundred years' time, or had buried some radioactive nuclear waste in an unsafe location. This act would harm many people who do not yet exist. If the above argument is correct, it would be wrong to say that their rights not to be harmed had been violated, for because they did not exist when the delayed-action bomb was planted they cannot be said to have any rights.

But this does not mean that planting the delayed-action bomb was not a very wicked thing to do. One has a moral obligation not to behave in a way that might inflict grievous harm on people, however removed from us they may be in time or space. We should reject the narrow view of rights according to which rights, and their counterpart obligations, exhaust the whole of morality. One can think of innumerable situations in which one's behavior will be influenced by some conception of what our moral obligations are, without necessarily believing that somebody or other must have some corresponding rights.

Intergenerational Justice and Equality

Because future generations don't have rights and certainly not a right to non-declining welfare, it is difficult to see how there can be any theory of intergenerational justice because almost all theories of justice confer rights. It is theoretically possible, however, to believe in the virtues of greater equality (between people at a point of time or between generations) without explicitly locating this belief in a systematic theory of rights and justice. Sustainable development is usually defended largely on the grounds of some unspecified notion of intergenerational equity. Now *equity* is not the same as *equality* because egalitarian principles are not the only possible kind of principles of equity. Nevertheless, most, if not all, theories of equity within generations contain, as a crucial ingredient, some appeal to the desirability of equality of something or other.[51]

Furthermore, most definitions of intergenerational equity include some reference to the desirability of equality between generations with regard to some specific variable, such as well-being, opportunity, or resources. For example, Goodin states that "considerations of intergenerational equity would demand . . . that each generation be guaranteed roughly equal benefits and insist that one generation may justly enjoy certain benefits only if those advantages can be sustained for subsequent generations as well" (1983: 13).

At first sight there seems to be a very simple and obvious objection to the notion that equality between generations can have any value: that most people probably hope that future generations are better off than we are. Similarly, most people probably feel rather pleased that we are far better off than were people in, say, the Middle Ages and do not suffer pangs of conscience about it. In other words, there seems to be a conflict between the objective of intergenerational egalitarianism and the goal of making future generations better off than we are.

But one important attempt to face up to this conflict has been made by Temkin, who writes that "Some worry that . . . egalitarianism has the counterintuitive implication that it is better not to want one's descendants to be better off than one's own generation, all other moral factors considered" (1995: 78–79, fn. 12). The crux of Temkin's defense against this view is that "the egalitarian's core belief is that it is unfair or unjust for some to be worse off than others *through no fault of their own*. It is *undeserved* or *nonvoluntary* inequalities that are morally objectionable" (1995: 78-9, fn.12). Given Temkin's conception of egalitarianism, according to which the unjust inequalities are those that are undeserved or involuntary, then "if we *want* our children or descendants to fare better than us, and voluntarily take steps to bring this about, there need be no objection to the resulting inequality" (1995: ibid).[52] In other words, if we take measures, such as save and invest, that will help make future generations richer than we are, there is no need for the egalitarian to complain because we are *voluntarily* making ourselves worse off than future generations will be *by voluntarily* taking steps to make them better off than we are.

This is all very well. But suppose future generations were expected to be richer than we are for reasons that are outside of our control. Suppose, for example, that future generations can be expected to become richer as a result of actions that we take today to raise our own living standards, which have the unintended consequence of also raising the standard of living of future generations. Most technological and scientific discoveries have this character. In this scenario, future generations might then be expected to be more prosperous than we are and hence have greater opportunities to pursue their conceptions of the good life than are open to people today. Thus, *through no fault of our own* we are poorer relative to future generations than we would otherwise be.

But if we regard natural inequalities as unjust, we would be morally obliged to take some action, however small after all things are considered, to reduce our poverty compared with future generations by, say, slowing down future growth (e.g., by investing less or using up more of the earth's supposedly scarce resources). However, most people—including me—would not want to slow down deliberately the future growth of welfare purely in the interests of intergenerational equality, and such a policy would certainly not appeal to proponents of sustainable development.

Quite apart from the apparent conflict between the desire to improve the welfare of future generations and the objective of intergenerational equality, one may ask what value does equality have anyway? Now this is a very old question that has been discussed for more than two thousand years, and this is not the place to go it into again, but the intergenerational context of sustainable development raises special problems for egalitarianism.

The most common grounds put forward for egalitarianism in general are instrumental grounds. That is to say, equality is widely believed to be good not so much in itself but on account of its alleged beneficial effects, such as reducing poverty, suffering, crime, social friction, and so on.[53] Similarly, one common argument in defense of equality of variables such as income or status or opportunity is that equality might promote a greater sense of social cohesion, greater productive efficiency, and so on, all of which may, in turn, promote welfare.

But it is difficult to transpose such instrumental advantages of egalitarianism to different *non-overlapping* generations. It is impossible, for example, for greater equality of incomes—or of anything else, for that matter—between *non-overlapping* generations to promote greater harmony between generations that do not coexist. In the same way, we cannot apply to generations that do not coexist the type of benefit of greater equality in certain aspects of life that Tawney eloquently names: reduction in envy, a greater sense of social solidarity and sense of community, and so on, brought about by greater equality that is "not equality of capacity or attainment, but of circumstances, institutions, and manner of life" (1964: 48).

Another common instrumental argument for greater equality is that great disparities of wealth or income eventually enable the rich to exercise undue power over the poor, leading perhaps to unacceptable inequalities of liberty. Clearly this, too, would not be feasible intergenerationally. And to the extent that poverty and suffering might be relieved by greater intergenerational equality, it is unfortunately the case that such relief would almost inevitably require transfers of wealth from future generations to the present generations, which, H.G. Wells aside, is a metaphysical impossibility.

If it is true that intergenerational equality can have no instrumental value, for reasons such as those set out above, then it can be defended only on the grounds that it has intrinsic value. That is to say, all values must be either instrumental or intrinsic.[54]

But it is surely implausible to suggest that there is any value to equality per se, for if equality were intrinsically valuable, it would make sense to promote it even by reducing the welfare of those who are better off without raising the welfare of the worse off. Most of us would not believe that this approach makes sense. If it were proposed that we achieve greater equality of incomes, for example, simply by taking some away from the rich, even though none of it would go to the poor—for example, it would all get lost through reduced incentives, bureaucratic procedures, and so on—few people would support such a move on the grounds of its intrinsic value.[55]

As Harry Frankfurt has succinctly put it, "The egalitarian condemnation of inequality as inherently bad loses much of its force, I believe, when we recognize that those who are doing considerably worse than others may nonetheless be doing rather well. . . . Inequality is, after all, a purely *formal* characteristic; and from this formal characteristic of the relationship between two items, nothing whatever follows as to the desirability or the value of either. Surely what is of genuine moral concern is whether people have good lives, and not how their lives compare with the lives of others" (1997: 5–6).

Resource Conservation and "Fairness" Between Generations

Most of the previous discussion in this chapter may seem to be too abstract and really rather irrelevant to the current fashionable concern with using up an "unfair" amount of the earth's resources. But we have no idea what the potential supply of resources is. Even if future generations were to be granted equal claims to allegedly finite resources, there is no useful sense in which one can identify what their equal claims actually amount to. It may be possible to identify the equal claim that all the inhabitants of a besieged city may have to a share in the available water and food supply. In this case, the participants know how much food and water there is as well as how many people there are. But in the case of resources and generations, if we were to share out finite resources over time equally on the grounds that everybody should have an equal share to the limited supply, we would have to share out the total potential supply of resource that will become available among all the people who will ever inhabit the earth, including those who are alive today.

The vast increases over the past in the estimates of supplies of some key resources have been shown in chapters 2 and 3. And we have no idea how the demand for different resources will change over the ages in the light of changing technology or of the changes that may take place in the development of substitutes, the pattern of output, tastes for different types of goods and services, and their relative prices. Furthermore, we have no idea how many people will eventually inhabit the earth anyway. The moral obligation not to condemn future generations to poverty by depriving them of essential resources is part of our natural duty to avoid inflicting unnecessary suffering on other people, but arguments presented in chapters 2 and 3 show that there is no need to fear that limited supplies of materials will constrain the future growth of incomes, so there is no need for the present generation to abandon its efforts to raise its own standard of living in order to fulfill this duty.

What Difference Does It All Make?

It might well be asked what difference it makes to practical policy whether one subscribes to the rights of future generations and to the dictates of intergenerational justice or, instead, falls back on the view adopted here: that we have only moral obligations to take account of the interests of future generations. I believe that it makes a profound difference because under any conception, rights—and the associated claims of justice—act as trumps over other mere interests. There are frequent conflicts in life between what actions might be thought to be in the general interest and somebody's rights—to freedom of choice in disposing or managing one's property or in working wherever one wants, to move to wherever one wants to live, and even, in many cases, to life and liberty. If future generations are to be accorded rights—for example, to inherit the environment as it now is or to be protected from any future decline in welfare from however high a level—these rights would trump the interests of people alive today, including the interests of the most deprived sections of the world population. As explained above, the ethical basis of sustainable development is precisely that future generations have rights that must take priority over the interests of preceding generations. By contrast, the perspective adopted here is to respect the interests that future generations will have, but not to give these interests any overriding priority. They have to be taken into account, along with the interests of people alive today, by trying to predict what the most important interests of future generations are likely to be and then, if there is a potential conflict, weighing them against the interests of present generations.

In other words, the interests of future generations are not to be ignored. On an "agent relative" ethical principle one might even accept that the interests of future generations should count less than those of people alive today. But even if they were to be given equal weight, this would not justify giving them some "trumping" power.

For the reasons set out in earlier chapters, future generations are on the whole highly likely to enjoy much higher living standards than those prevailing today. Of course, this rise in living standards will not ensure that all environmental problems will disappear, nor will it ensure that poverty will be eradicated everywhere—which is an impossible task. Generations ought not to be seen as homogeneous entities. At any moment of time, there will be poverty—and not just in some relative sense. So however prosperous future generations will be, this prosperity is unlikely to eliminate pockets of poverty altogether. By the end of this century, when average income levels should be at least four times as high as they are today, these problems will be greatly reduced, but today countless millions of people live in dire poverty and suffer the sickness and malnutrition and general destitution that acute poverty entails. It does not serve any concept of justice or deserve any moral praise if the immediate and known vital interests of people alive today are sacrificed in order to ensure that people alive in the year 2200 might be spared any decline in income below the level prevailing in the year 2190 or, even less, that they might be deprived of some of the several million species of beetles that are known to exist.

The moral policy, therefore, is to weigh up the interests of different generations. To do so, one must abandon the rights constraint and try to predict what will be the most important *interests* that future generations will have.

And the safest prediction that can be made for the future is that people will always want life, security, self-respect, and freedom from tyranny, oppression, and humiliation. Unfortunately, one can also safely predict that there will always be forces in society that will threaten these basic human wants. The twentieth century saw unparalleled violations of basic human rights throughout the world—on racial grounds, on religious grounds, on ideological grounds, and merely on the grounds that despots like to exercise their power. Thus, by contrast with the problems of widespread poverty or acute environmental problems, one problem will never be eradicated: the ever-present threat to basic human rights.

Conclusion

The greatest contribution that we can make to the welfare of future generations is to bequeath a free and democratic society. And the best means of bequeathing such a society to future generations is to improve respect for human rights and democratic values today. Because these rights are currently violated in most countries of the world, bequeathing a more decent and just society to future generations in no way conflicts with the interests of people alive today. There is no conflict between generations, therefore, with respect to the most important contribution that can be made to human welfare, and hence no trade-off is necessary between the interests of the present generation and the interests of future generations. There is no need for any grand new theory of intergenerational justice because justice is about the principles that should be applied in order to settle conflicts of interest in a peaceful manner. Where there are no conflicts—as David Hume pointed out centuries ago—there is no need for theories of justice. There is even less need, therefore, for any great new ethical insight or new guide to the best path of development for the human race, such as that claimed on behalf of the pathetically muddled principles of sustainable development.

Notes

1. A neat model of this kind is set out by Bruce Yandle (2000: 167–188], who compares it with the unholy alliance between bootleggers and Baptists during the Prohibition era in the United States, when the bootleggers had a vested interest in prohibition and well-meaning, if misguided, members of the public who had moral objections to the consumption of alcohol supported it also.

2. For a recent brief history of the development of the concept and its use in international conventions, see Lafferty and Meadowcroft 2000: chap. 1.

3. In a more recent paper, Pezzey (1997) indicates that the variety of definitions of sustainable development has proliferated enormously since his 1992 survey and provides a useful classification of three most common sustainability "constraints" encountered now in the literature.

4. See, for example, a recent study that emerged from the collaboration between the World Bank and the Centre for Social and Economic Research on the Global Environment (CSERGE), by Atkinson et al. (1997), which, in the introduction, defines sustainable development as nondeclining human well-being over time.

5. More precisely, the index, known as *2001 Environmental Sustainability Index,* was compiled by a team involving the Yale Center for Environmental Law and Policy and Columbia University's Center for International Earth Science Information Network, and it was presented at the annual meeting of the World Economic Forum, in Davos, Switzerland, January 2001.

6. The apparent mistake is that the report continually refers to the "sixty-seven" environmental indicators that are the basic building blocks of the final index, but the list of these variables in table 2 (main report, page 11) shows only sixty-six. However, in case there is some explanation for this discrepancy somewhere that I have been unable to locate, I refer to sixty-seven variables in the rest of this text.

7. The report does, however, point out that, in the end, the underlying sixty-seven variables do not finish up getting equal weight in the final ESI because unequal weights are implicit in the manner in which they are grouped in the higher-level twenty-two core indicators.

8. See references in the World Bank's *Report on the Limits to Growth*, mimeographed edition, Washington, D.C., September 1972, 38–39.

9. For a full list of sources, see Beckerman 1974: 274, n. 9.

10. Quoted in "Environmental Scares," in *The Economist*, 20 December 1997, 21–23.

11. Ibid, 22.

12. Figure based on world average compound rate of growth between 1950 and 1992 in Maddison, 1995: 212.

13. In Easterlin 1996 see a magisterial and optimistic study of the prospects for future growth in the light of a detailed analysis of the past.

14. Quoted in Streeten 1996, from Vidal's *Saving History* (Boston, Mass.: Harvard University Press, 1992).

15. Anderson 1998a, table 1 and page 8. Anderson's introductory note points out that the scenarios in question are still the subject of discussion in the relevant IPCC group and should not be interpreted as representing any final agreed consensus.

16. American Petroleum Institute 1995: 20. The estimates have also continued to rise. In 1994, the United States Geological Survey (USGS) estimated total recoverable oil reserves at between 1.4 and 2.1 trillion barrels, which corresponded to between sixty-three and ninety-five years of consumption at current rates of use (American Petroleum Institute 1995: 22). These USGS estimates exclude between 4 and 5 trillion barrels left in the ground as "unrecoverable." Later estimates (Rogner 1997) suggest an even higher figure, with total reserves representing approximately two hundred years' supply.

17. This prediction and some of the others quoted here are among the many such predictions listed in Mills 2000.

18. These fuel sources include, in particular, oil shale in the western United States, heavy and extra heavy oil of the kind found in Venezuela, and bitumen (natural tar) such as found in Alberta, Canada. If, as seems quite possible, market conditions and their resulting incentives to improve extraction and processing were to make these sources economically viable, they might add something in the region of 15 trillion barrels of oil. And even without some major rise in the price of conventional oil supplies, it is quite likely that they will become viable. For example, in Alberta there have been major cost reductions in recent years so that oil production

costs from these sources have fallen to approximately nine dollars per barrel, which, although much higher than the very cheap oil in the Middle East, is below the cost of North Sea oil and much lower than oil costs in most of the United States. If technological and market development brought a large proportion of these "unconventional" sources into the picture, then at current rates of consumption there would be enough oil to last for several centuries (American Petroleum Institute 1995, see esp. Table 5, p. 25).

19. Although the "further resources" in table 3 are estimates of reserves yet to be discovered and that might also be developed depending on costs and prices, they exclude what the originator of the estimates (Rogner) calls "additional occurrences" of fossil fuel reserves. These are resources that are known to exist but the size of which can only be guessed. It is believed that they may be at least 24,000 Gtoe, of which four-fifths are natural gas hydrates. If these additional resources were included, total resources would amount to approximately four thousand years' supply at current rates of consumption. So the human race still has plenty of time to think up something that will help prevent fossil fuel resources from being exhausted.

20. According to a recent review by Mock, Tester, and Wright, estimates for hot dry rock alone "are orders of magnitude larger than the sum total of all fossil and fissionable resources" (1997: 332). Although it is not yet known how much of these resources might be economically viable, the technological capacity for deep drilling already exists, so in principle it would be physically feasible to tap this resource. Insofar as the price of conventional fuels rose significantly, one can expect that there would be sufficient incentive for technical progress to be made in the exploitation of this source of energy.

21. Very similar conclusions are reached by Lomborg using data from different sources (See Lomborg, 2001: 133).

22. "Fuel Cells Meet Big Business," *The Economist*, 24 July 1999, 69–70. See also "Energy Survey," *The Economist*, 10 February 2001, 5–20, especially pages 15–16.

23. The potential for economically viable wind power fluctuates almost as much as the price of crude oil, and it is impossible to say now how far it is likely that such optimistic predictions will be born out in the future, but, from time to time, some favorable developments are reported, such as those in *The Economist*, 10 March 2001, 64–65.

24. See, for example, a critique of some popular exaggerated notions of the rate of destruction of forests in Stott 1999.

25. The eminent biologist Edward Wilson also surmised that the range might be between 10 million and 100 million and that "No one can say with confidence which of these figures is the closer" (1992: 330).

26. The U.S. Council of Environmental Quality and U.S. Department of State study entitled *The Global 2000 Report to the President* states that "An estimate prepared for the Global 2000 study suggests that between half a million and 2 million species—15 to 20 percent of all species on earth—could be extinguished by 2000" (1980: 37). Elsewhere (page 328 of the appendix) it is stated that the projection of species extinction was developed for the Global 2000 study by Thomas Lovejoy.

27. See Myers 1979 and Lovejoy's predictions contained in U.S. Council on Environmental Quality and U.S. Department of State 1980.

28. See, for example, the report in *The Economist*, 3 April 1999, 68. However, in some countries, notably Brazil, efforts have been made recently to remedy some of these failures (see *The Economist*, 12 May 2001, 12).

29. *The Economist*, 20 February 1999, 107.

30. See also Mendelsohn and Nordhaus 1996 for a particularly convincing demonstration that moderate global warming will, on balance, benefit U.S. agriculture. More recent estimates made both by the IPCC and the UK Meteorological Office (a leading world centre for climate change research) confirm the view that only if one accepts estimates of climate change near the top end of the range of possibilities specified by the IPCC is the net effect on global agriculture likely to be negative (see survey of their estimates in Lomborg, 2001: 287–291). However, there is general agreement that the effect on developing countries' agriculture is likely to be negative, offsetting to a greater or less extent (depending on the assumed rise in global temperatures) the gains in the developed countries.

31. Even Nordhaus's estimates have been challenged as being excessive, as in Goklany 2001.

32. See also IPCC 1990: xxv.

33. See also references to other more recent sources that confirm this assessment in Lomborg, 2001: 292-7.

34. This is confirmed in data going back to the beginning of the 20th Century in Lomborg, 2001: Fig. 154, p. 296.

35. See a very recent survey of this topic in Bradley 2000: 88–103.

36. Much of the material in the next few pages has been drawn from Morris 2000. For other international agreements embodying the precautionary principle, see also Miller and Conko 2000.

37. See Morris (2000, 16) for a nice summary of various ways in which we would all be deprived of many of the ingredients of our current standards of living that we now all take for granted.

38. *Financial Times*, 30 August 1997, 6; and United Nations Development Program (UNDP) 1998: 10.

39. The legal status of *Agenda 21* is far from clear, although it was later enshrined in a resolution of the Second Committee of the General Assembly of the UN (at its 51st meeting on 16 December 1992). But this resolution only urged governments and international bodies to take the action necessary to follow up the agreements reached in Rio, and there is no question of countries being brought before the International Court of Justice when they do not take much notice of it! After all, most countries in the world are constantly in breach of various more binding commitments into which they have entered concerning human rights, but they are never pursued in the courts or penalized in any way.

40. Draft report of the Committee on Natural Resources, Executive Summary, 12 February 1996.

41. Millions of people live in environments that are lacking the basic necessities of a decent existence. Poverty, not pollution, however, is the main cause of these poor environments.

42. For an extensive survey see Beckerman 1974: 160–68 and 1980.

43. See a good survey of this topic in Lafferty and Meadowcroft 2000: chap. 12.

44. Because the actions reported here took place before the GATT organization was replaced by the WTO, the references here retain the GATT designation.

45. Quoted in Berlin 1997: 242n who references Bowring, J. (ed). 1843. The Works of Jeremy Bentham, Volume 1. Edinburgh, p. 321.

46. It cannot be defended on egalitarian grounds, for example, because as drawn, the SD path actually shows more intergenerational inequality than does the MSW path!

47. This topic is discussed in far greater detail in Beckerman and Pasek 2001: chap. 2.

48. It should be pointed out that I am talking here about future generations of *unborn* people and am abstracting from the case of overlapping generations. Second, I am talking about *moral* rights, not legal rights. And, third, I do not wish to enter into a discussion of the general problem of how widely one should draw the boundary around the rights, if any, that

the present generation can be said to possess or the particular problem of how far these rights include rights over the environment.

49. I am here using the term *meaningless* to describe propositions such as "X is Y" when there is no X, although such propositions might be transposed into longer and clumsy propositions that are meaningful, such as "X exists, and if there is an X, it has Y," but are false if, in fact, there is no X.

50. This fundamental and in my opinion decisive point was made in De George 1981 and, if less forcibly, in Macklin 1981. But with some exceptions, notably de-Shalit 1995 and 2000: 137, it does not seem to have been given due weight in the literature on this subject. The same point is also set out very effectively in Merrills 1996: 31.

51. For example, both Rawls (1972) and Sen (1982, 1992) emphasize that equality of opportunity to pursue one's life goals is an essential feature of a just society. Others, such as Dworkin (1981), appeal to a suitably defined equality of resources as essential for distributive justice.

52. Temkin's discussion of this conflict of objectives is particularly useful here because he also explicitly abstracts from the issue of what it is exactly that egalitarians are concerned with, and he uses *welfare* as the focal variable for expositional convenience (see Temkin forthcoming).

53. For example, even the philosopher Hare's summary (1997) of the arguments for egalitarianism is essentially a simple utilitarian argument in terms of the extent to which greater equality would be instrumental in maximizing total utility. It is true that the utilitarian argument for maximizing utility can apply intergenerationally, up to a point, but if maximum utility requires transfers from later to earlier generations, as it is likely to do if the arguments in chapter 2 are correct, it is hardly a practical possibility.

54. Some objects may be bearers of both kinds of value. For example, flowers may be valued for their instrumental medicinal properties as well as for their intrinsic aesthetic value.

55. Those who did would probably be motivated largely by envy, which has no moral force, or by instrumental considerations, such as greater sense of social solidarity, which we have seen to play no role in intergenerational egalitarianism.

References

American Council on Science and Health. 1997. *Global Climate Change and Human Health*. New York: American Council on Science and Health.

American Petroleum Institute. 1995. *Are We Running Out of Oil?* Discussion Paper 081, Dec. Washington, D.C.: American Petroleum Institute.

Anderson, D. 1998a. *Explaining Why Carbon Emission Scenarios Differ.* Report for the Working Group III of the Intergovernmental Panel on Climate Change. London: Imperial College of Science and Technology.

———. 1998b. On the Effects of Social and Economic Policies on Future Carbon Emissions. *Mitigation and Adaptation Strategies for Global Change* 3: 419–53.

Atkinson, G., et al. 1997. *Measuring Sustainable Development: Macroeconomics and the Environment*. Cheltenham: Edward Elgar.

Ausubel, J. 1999. Five Worthy Ways to Spend Large Amounts of Money for Research on Environment and Resources. *The Bridge* 29(3): 4–16.

Balling, R.C., Jr. 1992. *The Heated Debate*. San Francisco: Pacific Research Institute for Public Policy.

Beckerman, W. 1974. *In Defence of Economic Growth*. London: Duckworth. (U.S. edition. *Two Cheers for the Affluent Society*. New York: St. Martin's, 1975.)

———. 1980. *Pricing for Pollution*. London: Institute for Economic Affairs.

———. 1992a. *Economic Development and the Environment*. World Bank Background Paper no. 24 to the World Development Report (1992). Washington, D.C.: World Bank.

———. 1992b. Economic Growth and the Environment: Whose Growth? Whose Environment? *World Development* 20, no. 4: 481–96.

Beckerman, W., and J. Pasek. 2001. *Justice, Posterity, and the Environment*. Oxford, Oxford University Press.

Bentham, C. 1997. Health. In *Economic Impacts of the Hot Summer and Unusually Warm Year of 1995*, edited by J. Palutikof, S. Subak, and M. Agnew, Norwich: University of East Anglia.

Berlin, I. 1997. *The Proper Study of Mankind*. London: Chatto and Windus.

Bhagwati, J. 1993. The Case for Free Trade. *Scientific American* 269 (Nov.): 17–23.

Bolin, B. 1997. Scientific Assessment of Climate Change. In *International Politics of Climate Change: Key Issues and Critical Actors*. edited by G. Fermann, 83–109. Oslo: Scandinavian University Press.

———. 1998. Key features on the Global system to be considered in analysis of the climate change issue. *Environment and Development Economics*, 3(3): 348–65.

Bradley, R. L., Jr. 2000. *Julian Simon and the Triumph of Energy Sustainability*. Washington, D.C.: American Legislative Exchange Council.

d'Auria, G., Tynan, N. Gillespie, C. and J. Thomas. 1999. *Property Rights and the Environment*. London: Institute of Economic Affairs.

De George, R. 1981. The Environment, Rights, and Future Generations. In *Responsibilities to Future Generations,* edited by E. Partridge, 157–166. New York: Prometheus.

de-Shalit, A. 1995. *Why Posterity Matters*. London and New York: Routledge.

———. 2000. The Environment Between Theory and Practice. Oxford: Oxford University Press.

Drèze, J., and A. Sen. 1989. *Hunger and Public Action*. Oxford: Oxford University Press.

———, eds. 1990. *The Political Economy of Hunger*. 3 vols. Oxford: Oxford University Press.

Dworkin, R. 1981. What Is Equality. Parts 1 and 2. *Philosophy and Public Affairs* 10: 185–246 and 283–345.

Easterlin, R. 1996. *Growth Triumphant: The Twenty-First Century in Historical Perspective*. Ann Arbor: University of Michigan Press.

Ehrlich, P., and A. Ehrlich. 1974. *The End of Affluence: A Blueprint for Your Future*. Rivercity, Mass.: Rivercity.

Esty, D., et al. 2001. *2001 Environmental Sustainability Index*. Davos, Switzerland: Global Leaders of Tomorrow Environment Task Force, World Economic Forum, in collaboration with the Yale Center for Environmental Law and Policy, Yale University, and the Center for International Earth Science Information Network (CIESN), Columbia University.

Faucheux, S., D. Pearce, and J. Proops, eds. 1996. *Models of Sustainable Development*. Cheltenham: Edward Elgar.

Frankfurt, H. 1997. Equality and Respect. *Social Research* 64, no. 1: 3–16.

French, A. 1964. *The Growth of the Athenian Economy*. London: Routledge and Kegan Paul.

Goklany, Indur M. 2001. *The Precautionary Principle: A Critical Appraisal of Environmental Risk Assessment*. Washington, D.C.: Cato Institute.

Goodin, R. 1983. Ethical Principles for Environmental Protection. In *Environmental Philosophy*, edited by R. Elliot and A. Gare, 3–20. Brisbane: University of Queensland Press.

———. 1994. Selling Environmental Indulgences. *Kyklos* 94: 573–96.

Grubb, M., and N. Meyer. 1993. Wind Energy: Resources, Systems, and Regional Strategies. In *Renewable Energy*, edited by T. Johansson et al. Washington, D.C.: Island.

Hare, R. 1997. Equality and Justice. In *Equality: Selected Readings*, edited by L. Pojmore and R. Westmoreland, 218–228. New York and Oxford: Oxford University Press.

Henderson-Sellers, A., et al. 1997. Tropical Cyclones and Global Climate Change: A Post-IPCC Assessment. *Bulletin of the American Meteorological Society* 79: 9–38.

Intergovernmental Panel on Climate Change (IPCC). 1990. *Climate Change: The IPCC Scientific Assessment*. Cambridge: Cambridge University Press.

———. 1996a. *Climate Change 1995, Impacts, Adaptation, and Mitigation of Climate Change: Scientific-Technical Analysis*. Contribution of Working Group II to the Second Assessment Report of the IPCC. Cambridge: Cambridge University Press.

———. 1996b. *Climate Change 1995: Economic and Social Dimension of Climate Change*. Contribution of Working Group III to the Second Assessment Report of the IPCC. Cambridge: Cambridge University Press.

———. 2001. *WG1 Third Assessment Report, Summary for Policymakers*. New York: United Nations.

Jevons, W. S. 1865. *The Coal Question*. London: Macmillan.

Lafferty, W. M., and J. Meadowcroft, eds. 2000. *Implementing Sustainable Development*. Oxford: Oxford University Press.

Lal, D. 1990. *The Limits of International Co-operation*. Twentieth Wincott Memorial Lecture. London: Institute of Economic Affairs.

———. 1997. Ecological Imperialism: The Prospective Costs of Kyoto for the Third World. In *The Costs of Kyoto*, edited by Jonathan Adler. Washington, D.C. The Competitive Enterprise Institute.

Landsea, C., Nicholls, N. Gray, W. and L. Avila. 1996. Downward Trend in the Frequency of Intense Atlantic Hurricanes During the Past Five Decades. *Geophysical Research Letters* 23: 527–30.

Lerchl, A. 1998. Changes in the Seasonality of Mortality in Germany from 1946 to 1995: The Role of Temperature. *International Journal of Biometeorology* 42: 84–88.

Lomborg, Bjorn. 2001. The Skeptical Environmentalist Measuring the Real State of the World. New York: Cambridge University Press.

Mabey, N., S. Hall, C. Smith, and S. Gupta. 1997. *Argument in the Greenhouse*. London and New York: Routledge.

Maddison, A. 1995. Monitoring the World Economy 1820–1992. Paris: OECD Development Center.

Macklin, R. 1981. Can Future Generations Correctly Be Said to Have Rights? In *Responsibilities to Future Generations,* edited by E. Partridge, 151–155. New York: Prometheus.

May, R. 1997. The Dimensions of Life on Earth. In *Nature and Human Society: The Quest for a Sustainable World,* edited by P. Raven and T. Williams. Washington, D.C.: National Academy Press.

———. 2000. The Florence Nightingale Lecture. Oxford: St. Anne's College.

Meadows, D. H., Meadows D.L., Randers J. and W.W. Behrens III. 1972. *The Limits to Growth.* A Report to the Club of Rome. New York: Universe.

Mendelsohn, R., and M.J. Balick. 1995. The Value of Undiscovered Pharmaceuticals in Tropical Forests. *Economic Botany* 49/2: 223–238.

Mendelsohn, R., and Ariel Dinar. 1999. Climate Change, Agriculture and Developing Countries: Does Adaptation Matter? *The World Bank Research Observer* 14/2: 277–93.

——— and Sanghi. 2001. The Effect of Development on the Climate Sensitivity of Agriculture. *Environment and Development Economics,* 6: 85–101.

Mendelsohn, R., and W. Nordhaus. 1996. The Impact of Global Warming on Agriculture—A Reply. *American Economic Review* 86/5: 312–15.

Merrills, J. 1996. Environmental Protection and Human Rights: Conceptual Aspects. In *Human Rights Approaches to Environmental Protection,* edited by A. Boyle and M. Anderson, 25–42. Oxford: Clarendon.

Miller, H. J., and G. Conko. 2000. Genetically Modified Fear and the International Regulation of Biotechnology. In *Rethinking Risk and the Precautionary Principle,* edited by J. Morris, 84–104. Oxford: Butterworth-Heinemann.

Mills, M. 2000. Renewable Energy and the Laws of Nature. Available online at http://www.fossilfuels.org/Electric/nature.htm, last accessed on Oct. 12, 2001.

Mock, J. E., J. W. Tester, and M. W. Wright. 1997. Geothermal Energy from the Earth: Its Potential Impact as an Environmentally Sustainable Resource. *Annual Review of Energy and the Environment* 22: 305–356.

Morris, J., ed. 2000. *Rethinking Risk and the Precautionary Principle.* Oxford: Butterworth-Heinemann.

Myers, N. 1979. The Sinking Ark. New York: Pergamon Press.

Nordhaus. W. 1994. *Managing the Global Commons.* Cambridge, Mass.: MIT Press.

Nordhaus, W. and Boyer, J. 2000. *Roll the Dice Again: Economic Models of Global Warming,* Cambridge, Mass.: MIT Press,

Norgaard, R. 1992. Sustainability and the Economics of Assuring Assets for Future Generations. World Bank Policy Research Working Paper WPS 832. Washington, D.C.: World Bank.

North, R. D. 2000. *Fur and Freedom: In Defence of the Fur Trade.* London: Institute of Economic Affairs.

Parfit, D. 1984. *Reasons and Persons.* Oxford: Oxford University Press.

Pezzey, J. 1992. *Sustainable Development Concepts: An Economic Analysis.* Environment Paper no. 2. Washington, D.C.: World Bank.

———. 1997. Sustainability Constraints Versus "Optimality" Versus Intertemporal Concern, and Axioms Versus Data. *Land Economics* 73, no. 4: 448–66.

Pigou, A. 1932. *The Economics of Welfare.* 4th ed. London: Macmillan.

Rawls, J. 1972. *A Theory of Justice.* Oxford: Clarendon.

Royal Commission on Environmental Pollutions (RCEP). 2000. *Energy: The Changing Climate.* London: Stationery Office.

Reiter, P. 1998. Global Warming and Vector-Borne Disease in Temperate Regions and at High Altitude. *The Lancet* 351: 839.

Ridley, M. 1995. *Down to Earth.* London: Institute of Economic Affairs.

———. 1996. *Down to Earth II.* London: Institute of Economic Affairs.

Rogner, H-H. 1997. *An Assessment of World Hydrocarbon Resources. Annual Review of Energy and the Environment* 22: 217–62.

Sandel, M. 1997. It Is Immoral to Buy the Right to Pollute. *New York Times,* 15 December.

Schelling, T. 1995. Intergenerational Discounting. *Energy Policy* 23, nos. 4–5: 395–401.

Schiesser, H., et al. 1997. Winter Storms in Switzerland North of the Alps. *Theoretical and Applied Climatology* 58: 1–19.

Sen, Amartya. 1982. Equality of What. In *Choice, Welfare, and Measurement*, 353–369. Oxford: Blackwell.

———. 1992. Inequality Reexamined. Oxford: Clarendon Press and New York: Russell Sage Foundation.

———. 1994. Population: Delusion and Reality. *New York Review of Books* (22 December): 62–71.

Stott, P. 1999. *Tropical Rain Forest: A Political Economy of Hegemonic Mythmaking*. London: Institute of Economic Affairs.

Streeten, P. 1996. Population Stabilizes, Economic Growth Continues? *Population and Development Review* 22, no. 4: 773–80.

Sugg, I., and U. Kreuter. 1994. *Elephants and Ivory: Lessons from the Trade Ban*. London: Institute of Economic Affairs.

Tawney, R. 1964. *Equality*. 5th ed. London: Unwin.

Temkin, L. 1995. Justice and Equality: Some Questions About Scope. *Social Philosophy and Policy Foundation* 12, no. 2: 72–104.

———. Forthcoming. Equality, Priority, and the Levelling Down Objective. In *The Ideal of Equality*, edited by M. Clayton and A. Williams. London and New York: Macmillan and St. Martin's.

't Sas-Rolfes, M. 1995. *Rhinos: Conservation, Economics, and Trade-Offs*. London: Institute of Economic Affairs.

UK Department of the Environment (DOE). 1996. *Indicators of Sustainable Development for the United Kingdom*. London: HMSO.

United Nations Development Program (UNDP). 1998. *Human Development Report*. New York and Oxford: Oxford University Press for the United Nations.

United Nations World Health Organization (WHO). 1998. *World Health Report 1998: Life in the 21st Century: A Vision for All*. Geneva: WHO.

U.S. Council of Environmental Quality and U.S. Department of State. 1980. *The Global Report to the President*. Vol. 2. Washington, D.C.: U.S. Council of Environmental Quality and U.S. Department of State.

Wilson, E. 1992. *The Diversity of Life*. London and New York: Penguin.

World Bank. 1997. *World Development Report (1997)*. Washington, D.C.: World Bank; Oxford: Oxford University Press.

World Commission on Environment and Development (WCED). 1987. *Our Common Future*. New York and Oxford: Oxford University Press.

Yandle, B. 2000. The Precautionary Principle as a Force for Global Political Centralization: A Case-Study of the Kyoto Protocol. In *Rethinking Risk and the Precautionary Principle*, edited by J. Morris, 167–88. Oxford: Butterworth-Heinemann.

Index

INDEPENDENT STUDIES IN POLITICAL ECONOMY

For further information and a catalog of publications, please contact:
THE INDEPENDENT INSTITUTE
100 Swan Way, Oakland, California 94621-1428, U.S.A.
510-632-1366 • Fax 510-568-6040 • info@independent.org • www.independent.org